LOST OKLAHOMA TREASURE

Misplaced Mines, Outlaw Loot & Mule Loads of Gold

W. CRAIG GAINES

Published by The History Press
Charleston, SC
www.historypress.com

Front cover: *W. Craig Gaines*.
Back cover, top: Fort Towson. *Oklahoma Historical Society*; *bottom*: Albert Pike. *Library of Congress*.

First published 2021

Manufactured in the United States

ISBN 9781467147897

Library of Congress Control Number: 2020948633

CONTENTS

INTRODUCTION

OKLAHOMA TREASURE

Ever since I was a young boy, I have been interested in history and lost treasure. Growing up in Oklahoma, I was fascinated by its diverse history and tales of lost treasure. Oklahoma was part of Native American, Spanish, French, Mexican, Texan and American lands.

I got my first metal detector when I was in junior high school and spent a lot of time digging up metal objects in my yard, other yards, school grounds and eventually the great outdoors of Oklahoma. Over the years, I traveled to all parts of Oklahoma on adventures of discovery, sightseeing and learning. In those years, I've researched and accumulated many tales and much historical information from a wide variety of sources.

The basis of these mostly legends were folk stories passed on by word of mouth from generation to generation. They usually have a basis of truth or at least someone's understanding of the truth. The early stories of lost gold and silver mines and the hiding of Spanish wealth are based mostly on stories developed by early settlers from the legacy of Hernán Cortés's conquest of Mexico. Evidence that Spanish explorers had been in Oklahoma came from Spanish arms and gear often found by ranchers and farmers.

Many stories came from newspaper accounts over the years. Some accounts are fiction conjured up by a writer for reader amusement, but others are factual. In the 1930s during the Great Depression, the Oklahoma Historical Society and larger Oklahoma newspapers gathered interviews with Civil War survivors and Oklahoma settlers. At that time, lost treasure stories were popular, and many Civil War and post–Civil War lost treasure stories were first put into print then. J. Frank Dobie's *Coronado's Children* was a collection of lost mines and lost treasure in the Southwest, including Oklahoma, that became a popular book.

Almost every family seems to have a lost treasure story associated with it. Sometimes a family member died without telling where he or she hid the family fortune or their egg money. Often a farmer plowing a field would mysteriously find scattered coins uncovered by the plow from some forgotten cache, such as my friend's family did.

Cherokees and a number of Native Americans learned about gold mining in Georgia during the great gold discoveries there that resulted in the United States taking their lands and removing them to Indian Territory in distant Oklahoma. When gold was discovered in California in 1848, the migration of would-be miners from the East through the Indian Nations on what became known as the California Road caused much excitement among the Cherokees. An internal destructive civil war between members of the Cherokees and other tribes over treaties signed by some tribal members with the United States caused some migration of tribal members to California to escape death threats and maybe to find gold. A few Cherokees were successful in finding gold in California and returned to the Indian Nations with it. Some of this gold still lies buried in Oklahoma. Successful miners returning east sometimes hid their gold during Indian and outlaw attacks.

The Civil War in Oklahoma devastated Indian tribes and nations who had established farms, ranches, schools, churches, mills and towns. A large number of people died during the war. About 28 percent of the Indians who served in the Union military died during the Civil War. Some left behind money that was never found. These Civil War treasure stories are true stories for the most part.

After the Civil War, many ex-soldiers did not adjust well to civilian life as farmers and cowboys. Some became outlaws who used the Indian Nations as a haven to hide out. Jesse James, Frank James and their relatives the Youngers formed the James Gang, which robbed banks, trains and citizens throughout the Midwest and left a lot of tales of buried treasure. The Knights of the Golden Circle were said to have been involved in some of these activities among die-hard ex-Confederates.

After the Civil War, the Indian Nations were reorganized as the United States took lands from the Five Civilized Tribes and gave it to other tribes or kept some lands as unassigned. Later, part of western Oklahoma became Oklahoma Territory and eastern Oklahoma became Indian Territory. Settlers were given homesteads and land rights on what had been Indian land. Railroads were constructed through these lands. Outlaw gangs on horseback carried out a number of robberies. The Dalton Gang, Doolin-Dalton Gang and others made their mark on Oklahoma. It is likely some outlaws left behind caches of loot before they met violent deaths. A number of small caches have been found in recent years. Many finds were based on so-called Jesse James maps that people acquired copies of.

One of my interests has been shipwrecks. There are still a few old shipwrecks in the Arkansas River and Red River in Oklahoma.

Much of this material came from my research for my books and articles. I have organized the treasure stories by county for ease of discussion and so the reader can locate treasure stories by geographic location. Some stories cover several counties, so I have put the story in one county and referenced it in the other county where it may be located. For most of these stories, I have tried to briefly tell the tale based on multiple sources. Steve Wilson's *Oklahoma Treasure and Treasure Tales* is one of the best sources for information on a number of these treasures. I have done my best to sort through the many versions of these treasure tales and give my opinion of them. The treasure values given in these stories are what legends have stated, but few lost treasures are actually worth millions of dollars.

I hope you get to visit the areas where these treasure tales take place. Enjoy the people and places in your travels like I have done. You might even find new treasure stories that I don't have in this book. With a bit of luck, you could become a treasure finder instead of a treasure hunter.

—W. Craig Gaines
Tulsa, Oklahoma
2020

CHAPTER 1

TREASURES BY COUNTY

ADAIR COUNTY

Farm Cache

A farmer hid his family's money on his farm near the Illinois River not far from Chewey. He died without telling anyone where it was. When I was young, I searched for it briefly with my first metal detector with the help of a friend whose family was from the area. The old homestead was long gone, and the directions were a bit vague about where the house originally was.

ATOKA COUNTY

Bill Cook's Lost Loot

See Johnson County.

John C. White Treasure

In the 1920s, rancher John White was rumored to have buried a quart jar full of five-, ten- and twenty-dollar gold coins close to his ranch house near Harmony, east of Atoka. He told W.F. McKown about burying the gold in

1923. White was leasing the ranch from others. White got sick and died in Texas. In 1960, some of John White's relatives came to the area and looked for their uncle John's money but did not appear to have found it.

BECKHAM COUNTY

Cavalry Payroll

See Cimarron County.

BLAINE COUNTY

Roman Nose Treasure

In 1874, a miner returning from Montana was said to have buried gold and silver coins in the Roman Nose State Park area near Eagle City. Another version of this tale was that $500,000 in gold coins was hidden during a Comanche raid in a canyon near the Washita River. The site was said to be about eight miles north of Watonga.

Yeager-Black Gang Treasure

A Yeager-Black Gang treasure was supposed to have been hidden near Eagle City. In 1895, outlaw Dick Yeager (also known as Nathanial Ellis "Zip" Wyatt) was killed in August and outlaw Isaac "Ike" Black was killed in in July in different gun fights.

See Major County, "Money in a Cave."

BRYAN COUNTY

Confederate Gold Chest

There is a local tale that in 1864 or 1865, a Confederate gold shipment traveled along the Blue River. As Union troops approached, the Confederates buried the chest of gold near the Red River. A steer's head was carved on a tree with one horn pointing up and one horn pointing down. The horn pointing down indicated where the chest was. The gold was supposedly hidden about three miles east of Highway 70 and about three miles east of Durant on Lone Oak Road. It was at the bottom of a hill on the edge of the Blue River.

About 1915, a young boy found the mysterious steer's head carving on the tree. He dug under the tree. After seeing an old Indian who lived nearby watching him, the young boy ran home. He returned to the site with his father. They discovered that the hole had been deepened by someone.

In the 1930s, the Newman brothers from Durant dug at the site with a steam shovel. Near a quicksand area, the steam shovel was said to have brought up an old rusted chest with the letters "C.S.A." on it. However, the chest rolled back into the quicksand. Upon resuming digging, they found the quicksand went down ninety feet, which exceeded the depth their steam shovel could dig. The Newman brothers gave up digging for the treasure.

Lost Cannon

Near Fort Washita, several cannons were reportedly buried. Another version of this story was that a cannon was put in a well.

Fort Washita. *Oklahoma Historical Society.*

Twenty-Seven Mule Loads of Gold

A legend claimed twenty-seven mule loads of gold were hidden in a creek near a large rock during an Indian attack. The site was near the mouth of the Little Wichita.

CADDO COUNTY

Fort Cobb Treasure

Two chests full of gold were said to have been buried near Fort Cobb.

Frank James Treasure

Outlaw Frank James reportedly hid $5,000 in gold and silver coins near a barn on the Billy Royce Farm near Anadarko in the Keechi Hills. He may have recovered it. Other counties with James Gang treasure, both lost and found, are Comanche, Grady, Jefferson, Kay, Le Flore, Mayes, Rogers and Tulsa.

See Comanche County, "James Gang $2 Million Cache and Other Caches."

Lost Platinum Mine

Prospector A.S. Keown was murdered in 1924 between Anadarko and Fort Cobb with a bullet in his head by an unknown attacker. After he died, it was discovered that he had been selling platinum scrapings to an Oklahoma City jeweler. Some thought the platinum was from a mine that he accessed from his cabin on the George Thomas Ranch about fifteen miles northwest of Meers. This mine was said to be in the Keechi Hills, but he did not own the land. Keown had been working to buy the land or get the mining rights just before he was murdered. The Bat Cave in the area has been mentioned as a possible site with a secret room under water, but this seems unlikely.

Spanish Treasure

A Spanish treasure worth $200,000 in gold coins was rumored to be hidden near Cement.

Fort Cobb. *Oklahoma Historical Society.*

Frank James. *Library of Congress.*

CARTER COUNTY

Gold-Stuffed Cannon

Spaniards were said to have stuffed two gold bars and four silver bars into a cannon and hid it near Ardmore on Hickory Creek. In another story, it was Confederates being attacked by Indians who lost their cannon in Hickory Creek. The location of some sort of battle associated with this tale is S/2 Section 25 T5S-R1E.

CHEROKEE COUNTY

Blackface Treasures

In the 1830s, a renegade Black Seminole called Blackface led a gang that looted traders, pack trains and settler wagons. Seminole Indians had been removed from Florida to present Oklahoma by the U.S. Army after the many years of fighting the United States. This story likely was based on some exiled Seminoles who continued to resist in Indian Territory.

Mexican traders traveling from Mexico bound for St. Louis with several mule loads of gold were reportedly ambushed by Blackface's gang near where the Fort Gibson National Cemetery is located. All the traders were killed. The gold was hidden in a cave by a few gang members. Blackface and his band were all hunted down and killed.

This treasure was forty large gold bars hidden a half-day's ride from Tahlequah. In the 1920s, a Cherokee man searching for the gold agreed to give an innkeeper half the treasure if the innkeeper would let him stay for a month while he searched for it. Just before the stay was over, the man found the cave and treasure. He took the blindfolded innkeeper to the site. The cave entrance was concealed by rocks. The Cherokee removed the rocks and used a torch to enter the cave. Inside, several large clay jars contained small gold bullion bars. They took only one gold bar and left the cave. The innkeeper was again blindfolded on the way out. The next morning, the Cherokee disappeared, as he had killed someone and the police were after him. The innkeeper searched for the cave and never found it.

Another version of this story was that a man found a treasure in coins about fifteen miles south of Tahlequah near Qualls but covered it up and planned to return later to retrieve it. He got sick and died.

See Latimer County, "Wilburton Outlaw Caches" for another Blackface treasure.

Park Hill/Murrell Mansion. *Library of Congress.*

Cherokee Silver Mine

A legend indicated that Cherokees hid a silver mine near Park Hill. This story ties into a tale about Uncle Billy Melton, who was with his dog near Park Hill when the dog chased a rabbit into a crevice in a bluff. Getting a stick, Melton tried to get the rabbit out of the crevice. Instead, what was described as a solid chunk of silver came out. Since no mining was allowed in the Cherokee Nation, Melton never did anything about the find. This story came from Reverend Walter A. Duncan, who was Cherokee Chief John Ross's secretary. I suspect what he found was iron pyrite (which is found in shales or other rocks), or it may have been lead or zinc, which is found in sedimentary rock in northeast Oklahoma in Mississippian age carbonates that outcrop in the area.

Flowers Canyon Treasure

A group of Spaniards may have buried treasure in Flowers Canyon a couple miles northeast of Fort Gibson. Indians had attacked the Spaniards, who left their treasure behind. Dresser Cave, located about four miles northeast of Fort Gibson, is associated with this legend. Dresser Cave is named after a man who moved into the cave in 1913, lived there about four years and disappeared. Dresser Cave is on the south side of the canyon about forty feet above Flowers Creek. It is about fifteen feet wide and six feet in height.

Heirloom Treasure

Before the Civil War, three escaped slaves were said to have fled from Mississippi across Arkansas to the Cherokee Nation. They took some of their master's gold and heirlooms. Their master and a posse pursued them. Near the Illinois River east or southeast of Tahlequah, the posse caught up with the escaped slaves. One fugitive slave was shot, and the others were captured. They did not have the gold or heirlooms on them. They were believed to have hidden the treasure in a hollow tree near a chimney-shaped rock.

Horseshoe Bend Treasure

In the mid-1800s, some Cherokees supposedly hid gold bars in a couple of earthen churns in a cave in a valley in the Illinois River Horseshoe Bend area. These gold bars could have been from Cherokees who mined gold in the California gold rush. Some Cherokees returned back to the Cherokee Nation with gold.

John N. Riley's Treasure

Cherokee John N. Riley lived on a farm six miles east of Fort Gibson before the Civil War. Afraid of being robbed, he buried his family's prized possessions, including their silverware, near his farm. Riley died before he disclosed where the treasure was hidden to his family.

Joseph Henry Clark's Treasure

Before the Civil War, farmer Joseph Henry Clark lived in the Park Hill area. He was said to have buried somewhere near his farmhouse $5,000 in gold coins from selling slaves and property. In 1865, while traveling on the Fort

Illinois River. *Oklahoma Historical Society*.

Gibson Military Road between Park Hill and Fort Gibson, he was ambushed and murdered. One of his descendants, Admiral Joseph James "Joko" Clark, was the first Cherokee to graduate from the U.S. Naval Academy and became a navy admiral. A January 22, 1945 *Life* magazine article on Admiral Joseph James Clark said the Clark family and neighbors were still looking for Grandpa Clark's buried treasure.

Lost Cherokee Nation Treasures

There is a legend that just before the Civil War, the U.S. government paid $50,000 in gold coins to the Cherokee Nation. Four Cherokees were put in charge of the gold, which was placed in two nail kegs. The two kegs were then hidden on Tahlequah Creek. It may have been buried behind the Cherokee capitol building, half a mile south on Tahlequah Creek within sight of the capitol. The Civil War was extremely violent, with many Cherokees dying in combat as well as by illness. At the end of the Civil War, only one of the original four Cherokee trustees who hid the gold survived. The Cherokee trustee gave directions on the treasure's location to Cherokee council members. In spite of their efforts to recover the treasure, they could not find it.

Cherokee Nation capital Tahlequah. *Library of Congress.*

Chief John Ross.
Oklahoma Historical Society.

The Cherokee capitol building was burned down in 1863 by Confederate Cherokee Colonel Stand Watie and his Confederate Indians. A new capitol was constructed on the site of the old building and now serves as part of the Cherokee Nation's offices.

Another version of the story was that the kegs were buried near the village of Park Hill, where Chief John Ross and other Cherokee Nation leaders lived. Another related story claimed a wagonload of silver was sent by the Union for Chief John Ross to convince him to support the Union cause. The wagon overturned and was lost in the Illinois River just south of the Barren (Baron) Fork in the spring of 1862.

The truth is that Chief John Ross had from $70,000 to $80,000 of the Cherokee treasury when he was escorted by part of the Union Sixth Kansas Cavalry Regiment from Park Hill on August 3, 1862. The Cherokee Nation treasury was taken to Kansas. Chief John Ross went in exile to Philadelphia and Washington, D.C. It is highly unlikely there is any lost Cherokee Nation treasury gold or silver, but some small caches are possible.

Joe Payne Silver Mine

U.S. deputy marshal Joe Payne lived south of Tahlequah and spent a lot of time tracking down outlaws in Indian Territory. One day, he went hunting in the Cherokee Hills and sat down by a stream, where he took off a boot and shook gravel out of it. Suddenly, he noticed a large vein of silver about three feet wide that went under the stream and exited on the other side. The Cherokee Nation did not allow mining. To hide the vein, he cut down some trees and laid them over the vein. He later returned and dug down into the vein and found it to be at least four feet thick. He never tried to mine the silver and died in 1904. Payne did make a map of how to find the silver vein and gave it to a good friend. His friend did not find the site. Payne's friend later gave the information to a friend's brother-in-law, who did not find the site. It is possible this was lead or zinc rather than silver.

Rich Joe Vann Treasure

The richest Cherokee before the Civil War, Joseph "Rich Joe" Vann, was driven out of his Georgia plantation called Diamond Hill at Spring Place, Georgia, during Indian Removal. Rich Joe Vann died in 1844 when his steamboat, the *Lucy Walker*, blew up during a steamboat race. Vann's steamboat was named after his favorite racehorse. There is a legend that Rich Joe Vann buried $60,000 in gold before leaving on his last voyage on the *Lucy Walker*. Vann's mansion was at the town of Webbers Falls on the Arkansas River. His lands and wealth passed on to his family, including his son, who served both in the Confederate Drew's Regiment of Cherokee Mounted Rifles and Union Kansas Indian Home Guard. During the Civil War, Webbers Falls was the site of skirmishes in 1863. The Confederate Cherokee Council also held several meetings in Webbers Falls. Union soldiers burned down the Vann Mansion as none of the Vann family reportedly would disclose where Confederate gold was buried nearby.

Robin Bobb's Treasure

A June 28, 1931 *Tulsa World* article related the tale of Robin Bobb's treasure. Cherokee Robin Bobb was the son of Jim Bobb. Jim Bobb, like a number of Cherokees, had gone to California during the gold rush in the 1850s and returned with some gold. Robin Bobb inherited some of those California gold coins from his father. Robin was thrifty and saved his money. He farmed and raised cattle. The local story was that he took his treasure on horseback into the woods to a narrow valley ten miles east of Tahlequah called Baumgarner Hollow near the Illinois River. He hid his coins in a heavy bag in an iron cooking pot. Several people saw him return home and said he was wet up to his shoulders. This indicated he likely crossed the nearby Illinois River. At the time, they thought he had gone hunting, as he had his shotgun and a dead wild turkey when he returned. Like most Cherokees, he left the area during the Civil War as a refugee. Robin Bobb returned to the area after the war but died before he could recover his treasure.

Stinnett Treasure

William (Uncle Billy) Stinnett had a prosperous trading post in southeast Park Hill on the road to the Illinois River. Stinnett was said to have hidden his money nearby. He came to the area with his wife in 1828. He was a trader for about fifty years. When he died in 1838, his money was missing, so people believed it was still hidden. It was thought to be near the ford on a road on the Illinois River.

One version of this story reported Stinnett's widow was a cripple. A young man married her for her money. She died shortly afterward without telling her new husband where her money was hidden.

Tom Hicks Treasure

During the Civil War, Cherokee Tom Hicks buried about $600 near his farm. His farm was near where the Kansas, Oklahoma and Gulf Railroad would later cross the Grand River in Mayes County or Cherokee County. Tom Hicks was a Union sympathizer who likely was a member of the Pins, who wore pins on their lapels. Confederates murdered him. The location of his treasure went with him to his grave.

A March 1967 article published in *The Artifact* with the title "Tom Hicks $600 Waits No More" by an anonymous writer related how he found Tom Hicks's lost treasure. He had talked to some locals at Strang and got information to locate Hicks's farm. It was six miles north of Strang. After parking his car, the treasure hunter walked a half mile or so to a bluff overlooking the Grand

River. The foundations of the old house were visible, as were trees that had been planted. Using a metal detector for three hours, he found nothing of note. He then wondered where Tom Hicks got his water since his house was on a bluff. He noticed cottonwood trees about seventy-five yards from the house foundation. He found evidence of a rocked-up spring among the trees and got a loud signal at the stump of an ancient cottonwood tree. On his third shovel full of dirt, coins appeared. He recovered twenty-five $20 gold coins, four $10 gold coins and one $5 gold coin—a total of $515 in old gold coins. He dug down two feet farther and found nothing more. Going over the area with his metal detector, he got no signals. He left quickly with his newly found treasure.

Williams Cache

Buffalo Head Williams was a former U.S. Army soldier in 1828 or 1829 and a farmer who became a U.S. government worker. Williams grew fruit on his farm about a mile north of Tahlequah. He was called Buffalo Head Williams due to his curly hair. Williams supposedly hid an iron chest with thousands of dollars in silver and gold coins near his house before the Civil War. After the Civil War, people searched for the treasure without anyone claiming to have found it. A family cemetery, orchard and blacksmith shop were said to have been on his property.

CHOCTAW COUNTY

Boggy Creek Treasure

A legend claimed an outlaw treasure was hidden on Boggy Creek near Boswell.

Confederate Gold and Silver

Confederate gold and silver were rumored to have been buried not far from Fort Towson near Doaks Trading Post on the Red River. The gold and silver came from mines in Arizona, New Mexico, Colorado or California and was headed for a Confederate mint. This story is very suspect, as the Confederacy minted very few coins during the Civil War.

Fort Towson. *Oklahoma Historical Society.*

Found Bucket of Treasure

Headlines and an article in April 1971 told the story of a couple of successful treasure hunters with a metal detector finding an old rusty bucket with about $3,000 in coins (minted 1850 to 1881), which could be worth $30,000. The find consisted of more than 202 silver dollars, 79 $20 gold pieces, 53 $10 gold pieces, 43 $5 gold pieces and two $2.50 gold pieces. The treasure was found at an old Butterfield Stage station north of Hugo. The Butterfield Stage Road ran from Fort Smith, Arkansas, to Colbert's Ferry on the Red River, with twelve stations spaced along the way. The stage ran from 1857 to 1861.

This treasure was found by Charles E. Coker of Hugo and his brother-in-law W.F. Tyler from Fort Worth, Texas. It was buried a foot below ground. The metal detector had a weak signal because of a low battery, so the treasure was almost missed. Coker had borrowed the metal detector from his dad. Since he found the coins with a D-Tex Standard metal detector, a picture of Coker and his treasure find was featured in D-Tex Electronics ads in treasure hunting magazines.

CIMARRON COUNTY

Cavalry Payroll

A U.S. cavalry force reportedly was transporting a $42,000 payroll to Fort Supply in 1868 when Kiowa Chief Little Wolf and his band were said to have attacked the cavalry soldiers and killed them. The soldiers (or a cavalry officer) buried the payroll in the Oklahoma Panhandle on the Golf River about two miles south of Sturgis. A campsite found in the 1870s east of Kerrick, Texas, on the Canadian River was their last camp before they headed east into Oklahoma. One version of this tale said that the payroll was hidden between Soldier Springs and old Ural in Beckham County.

Frenchmen's Gold

In about 1800, a twelve-man French party was in Mexico, where they were said to have stolen gold from placer miners and murdered as many as twenty miners. This was about the time when France regained Louisiana from Spain. The Frenchmen were in northern New Mexico in the Santa Fe–Taos area, where they panned for gold in Colfax County. Six Frenchmen died before the party finally left for Louisiana. They reportedly transported about five hundred ingots weighing seventy-five pounds each on six carts down the Santa Fe Trail. Fearing the Americans who just bought Louisiana would seize their gold, the Frenchmen headed back to Santa Fe. Indians attacked them. Only one man survived.

Another version of this tale was that in the late summer of 1804, a Spaniard and seven Frenchmen with six carts with five hundred gold ingots headed for New Orleans. They traveled on the Cimarron Cutoff of the Santa Fe Trail. The caravan stopped at Flag Spring (also called Upper Spring), where they camped and got water. Four mountain men told them Louisiana had become a U.S. territory when France sold it to the United States in 1803. Two Frenchmen left the others behind and headed toward New Orleans to determine if they should take the gold to the U.S. territory. This tale was detailed in Spaniard Jose Lopat's Bible. Lopat was a guide and metalworker from Santa Fe who did not own any of the gold. Lopat had molded the five hundred gold ingots. He returned to Santa Fe and wrote down information on his adventure.

One Frenchman, an ex-priest turned outlaw called Pierre LaFarge, supposedly made his way back to Santa Fe. LaFarge had been excommunicated for murdering a nun and spent time in prison. He had tuberculosis and was a hunted man by relatives of the miners the Frenchmen had murdered. LaFarge told Lopat that the others in the party had died. LaFarge then fled from Santa Fe, dying a couple of weeks later. Lopat went to search for the gold at Flag Spring but did not find it. He died in 1856. His son, Emmanuel Lopat, later put these notes into the Lopat family Bible. This Bible was later found by his relatives, who looked for the treasure.

Stone markers thought to be related to the treasure are on the Cy Strong Ranch near Boise City. There were several interpretations as to where the gold was cached. In 1878, rocks were found imbedded in the soil about a quarter mile long, forming a rough square with four markers. The area within the markers is about thirty-six square miles, with Sugar Loaf Peak in the middle. Four sets of stones, each in the form of a Roman numeral, were found miles apart. The gold ingots were supposed to be hidden somewhere near Flag Spring and Sugar Loaf Peak, northwest of Boise City. Lots of people have searched for this site, including Steve Wilson, who wrote a book and articles on it. It is unlikely markers for this type of treasure would cover so large a search area.

Hidden Outlaw Loot

Between 1870 and 1880, outlaws were rumored to have stolen $80,000 from a West Texas bank and hidden it in a cave near Casteneda. Texas Rangers chased the outlaws and killed two of them. Of the surviving remaining outlaws, one was wounded and later died. The outlaws put their loot in a cave along with their comrade's body in the gyp sinks. They hid the cave entrance with rocks. These two outlaws were later killed.

Two boys—Ed Power, fourteen, and Marvin Walton, twelve—found a small cave with rocks covering the entrance. They removed the rocks and found a skeleton in old clothes with old bags containing shiny objects in the cave. A large rattlesnake in the cave chased them out. They did not tell anyone about their discovery for several years. When they were older, they were unable to relocate the cave.

Reynolds Gang Treasures

The Reynolds Gang started out as a Confederate guerrilla band from Texas. The gang was organized by "Colonel" Jim (James) Reynolds and his brother John Reynolds in 1864. The Reynolds Gang assembled at Las Vegas, New Mexico Territory, with plans to raid Union gold and silver shipments in the Southwest. The gang numbered twenty-three men when it was said to have robbed a wagon train en route from Chihuahua, Mexico, to Santa Fe, New Mexico Territory, of $60,000 in newly minted gold. Lieutenant George L. Shoup of the Union Colorado volunteers wrote that the Reynolds Gang had in fact robbed a wagon train of $1,800 in specie in New Mexico Territory and about the same amount in currency. Victims of the robbery reported that they lost $10,000 and forty mules to the Confederate guerrillas.

Jim Reynolds wanted to cache the loot and retrieve it later for the Confederacy. Most of the Reynolds Gang wanted the gold to be divided up among the gang members. Finally, in the Sangre de Cristos, Jim Reynolds divided up the loot and gave each a share. Near Spanish Peaks, Colorado, it was reported the remaining members of the Reynolds Gang buried their shares (which may have totaled $22,500) of their robberies, likely in Colorado or New Mexico. Most Reynolds Gang members left with their loot, leaving only a few to follow Jim Reynolds into Colorado. Union Lieutenant Shoup reported that gang members took their loot to Fort Belknap, Texas, and divided it up there.

Lieutenant Shoup's report in the "Official Records" claims, "They say that no money was cached on the Cimarron or elsewhere by them." This sounds like some of the Reynolds Gang cached loot on the Cimarron River or the Cimarron Branch of the Santa Fe Trail and lied to Shoup, and he knew it.

Reynolds Gang member Tom Holliman (Holderman) was captured in Colorado and said they hid money. It is not likely that all of their buried loot was recovered. All the members of the Reynolds Gang who went to Colorado were killed except for John Reynolds, Jake (Jack) Stowe and John Anderson. After committing a series of Colorado robberies, the Reynolds Gang members were not treated as Confederate irregular soldiers, which is what they seem to have considered their role. Several Reynolds Gang members were executed without trial by Union soldiers. The Confederacy used irregular units and soldiers during the Civil War. The Confederate Secret Service files were destroyed at the end of the war, so it is hard to prove which irregulars actually had Confederate army commissions.

Robbers Roost

Robbers Roost is an elevated point called Lookout Peak about half a mile from Black Mesa. Black Mesa has an elevation of about five thousand feet and is the highest point in Oklahoma. It is about four miles northeast of Kenton near Lookout Point on the Elzy Tanner Place. The outlaw hideout was on the east bank of Carrizzo Creek (Carozzo Creek or Rio Carrizo). It was a rock house sixteen feet by thirty-six feet with thirty-inch-thick walls with gun loopholes. Stone fireplaces were at either end of the structure. Captain Bill Coe was the leader of forty to fifty men who raided the Santa Fe Trail and area ranches from Robbers Roost.

The Coe Gang may have been part of an irregular Confederate force like the Reynolds Gang. Robbers Roost was reportedly blown up by Union forces with a six-pounder cannon after 1863, perhaps in 1865. Union forces under General Kit Carson established Camp Nichols about five miles northeast of Mexona in May 1865 along the Cimarron Cutoff of the Santa Fe Trail. Camp Nichols protected wagon trains between Kansas and Santa Fe, New Mexico Territory. Union troops escorted wagon trains in both directions. This post had several mountain howitzers that could have been used to demolish Robbers Roost.

Another version of this story was that the Coe Gang stole U.S. Army livestock from Fort Union, New Mexico Territory, and Fort Lyon, Colorado Territory, after the Civil War. In 1867, U.S. Army troops attacked Robbers Roost with a cannon and demolished it after killing several robbers. At Folsom, New Mexico Territory, Coe was said to have been captured by U.S. Army soldiers in July 1868 and put in the Pueblo, Colorado Territory jail. A mob pulled him out of the jail and hanged him on July 21, 1868. Some loot may have been hidden in the Robbers Roost area by the Coe Gang.

Santa Fe Trader's Money

In 1828 a party of 25 American traders with five wagons and 150 mules and horses left Santa Fe after a very profitable and successful trading expedition. They were reportedly transporting $50,000 in Mexican silver coins back home. They were two weeks behind a larger American trading party that had left Santa Fe for the United States. The first party was larger than the second party. The first party of traders were attacked by Comanches, but successfully made it back to Missouri after losing a few men. The second party went down the Cimarron Cutoff portion of the Santa Fe Trail through the Oklahoma Panhandle.

One version of this story was as the second party reached Upper Spring (also called Flag Spring) they found hostile Indians (likely Comanches) already camped there. The traders circled their wagons and held off the Indians near what presently is a park on Highway 287. They moved five miles east the next day and were said to have buried most of their silver coins before heading toward Chouteau's Island, Kansas Territory as the Indians attacks continued.

Another more detailed version was that Comanches started stealing their mules and horses and harassed them all along the Cimarron Cutoff. At least one trader was killed. Near the present Oklahoma – Colorado, Kansas border they ran out of livestock and could no longer move their wagons. In desperation each trader took about $1,000 in silver coins and what food and water he could carry. They escaped at night with about $24,000 in silver coins. They left about $26,000 behind. Whether it was buried all together at some place or whether each man buried his share at a different spot was not disclosed in this tale.

The coins were heavy and the traders were still harassed by mounted Indians along their way toward home. They reached Chouteau's Island on the Arkansas River where they cached most of their silver coins as they were running out of strength and food. The traders continued walking down the Santa Fe Trail until they ran into other Americans who formed a relief party that rescued most of the traders. Some traders died before they could be rescued. Likely the survivors recovered their silver coins, but some coins hidden in individual hiding caches may still remain in Oklahoma, Colorado, and Kansas. Another possibility is that the Indians took the Mexican silver coins the traders had cached. The 1829 American trading expedition to and from Santa Fe had U.S. Army and Mexican Army escorts to prevent Indian attacks.

COAL COUNTY

Bandit Treasure

A bandit treasure may have been hidden on Delaware Creek. This also could be Bill Cook's lost loot or the James Gang loot in Johnson County.

Bill Cook's Lost Loot

See Johnson County.

COMANCHE COUNTY

Cutthroat Gap Treasures

At or near Cutthroat Gap in the Wichita Mountains, a U.S. Army payroll of $96,000 in gold coins was said to have been hidden. This is likely the Kiowa County, Otter Creek Treasure or even a James Gang treasure. Cutthroat Gap is the site where Osages massacred a party of Kiowas and cut off their heads in 1833. One of the Kiowas may have had silver coins taken from a Santa Fe traders' expedition in the Texas Panhandle. His coins were said to have been buried at Cutthroat Gap. Some coins have been found in the area over the years.

Fort Sill Treasures

In about 1892, bandits reportedly robbed a stage in southern Oklahoma of $100,000 (four bags of gold and two bags of silver coins) in loot. The robbers threw the loot down the Fort Sill Trading Post's well or buried it near a well near the Fort Sill Post Trader Store near the corner of McBride Avenue and Cureton Avenue. The well was later filled in.

One of the bandits called Allen was badly wounded after the robbery. He was captured and sent to prison in Huntsville, Texas. After thirty-five years, he came back to Fort Sill to recover his loot, but the military post had changed. The army guards chased him off the post. Allen became ill and told his friend G.W. Cottrell of Levelland, Texas, the story of the robbery and hidden loot. Cottrell got permission to look for the loot, but they found nothing. In April 1964, Fort Sill personnel used an earth auger to dig some holes around the old well, but they never found any treasure.

Other outlaws supposedly stole $40,000 from a Wichita, Kansas bank and also hid it near Fort Sill.

Fort Sill. *Author's photo.*

James Gang $2 Million Cache and Other Caches

A legend claimed the James Gang hid $2 million in gold bullion (gold ore and gold nuggets taken from a wagon train) in the Wichita Mountains on the west foot of Twin Mountain on the road between Fort Sill and the Keechi Hills not far from Cache Creek. One version of this story claimed that in the 1870s, Frank James, Jesse James and their gang robbed a Mexican wagon train carrying $500,000 in gold bound to finance a Mexican revolution. This legend is in J. Frank Dobie's book *Coronado's Children*. There were several stories as to where this much money came from. Some said the buried cache was from the numerous bank, train and other robberies committed by Jesse James, Frank James and their gang members.

Another story was that in 1875, a Mexican treasure pack train containing eighteen burros traveling through Oklahoma on its way to St. Louis, Missouri, was robbed. Another variation said the robbery took place in Mexico across the Rio Grande from El Paso, Texas. In February 1876, the James Gang was supposed to have ambushed a twenty-burro train carrying $2 million. They killed the guards and handlers. The burros and the $2 million were driven across the Rio Grande to Texas. They drove the treasure train north and entered Indian Territory on March 1. On March

4, they camped on Cache Creek near present Cement. On a bucket, they wrote the names of all the gang members and put it in the ground with some other items. The gold ingots were buried in a deep hole nearby. They put rocks over the location and hammered a burro shoe into a cottonwood tree to be a treasure marker. The burros were turned loose, and the gear for the burros were burned and buried.

Yet another version of this story is it was a possible Knights of the Golden Circle treasure worth $8 million (Mexican gold coins) from Emperor Maximillian's payment to Jesse Woodson James (also known as J. Frank Dalton), as recited in *Rebel Gold*. Steve Wilson's *Oklahoma Treasure Lost and Found* collected a lot of information on the James Gang treasures and those who searched for them.

Although most members of the James Gang were killed or imprisoned, Frank James surrendered to the justice system and managed to escape going to prison but spent some time in jail. After being acquitted of charges in Missouri, Frank James worked at a variety of jobs over the years in Louisiana, Missouri, Texas and Washington. He bought a 160-acre farm on Cache Creek near Fletcher and settled down with his wife, Ann. The farm was northeast of Lawton between U.S. 277 and the H.E. Bailey Turnpike. Fletcher is close to Cement, where the James Gang members were supposed to have hidden $2 million in gold. Frank James searched extensively for hidden James Gang treasures in the area and recovered $6,000 east of Cement and at least one other cache. Some thought he recovered as many as fourteen different caches.

Jesse James. *Oklahoma Historical Society*.

Frank James also looked for treasure hidden near the Western Cattle Trail from Fort Griffin, Texas, to Dodge City, Kansas. The James Gang were said to have buried $200,000 near a trail, maybe the Western Cattle Trail, with several locations mentioned between Fort Sill and Lawton on Cache Creek ($92,000 by one account) in the Keechi Hills between 1867 and 1882. (See Jefferson County, "Addington Treasure.") The land had changed in the years since the loot was buried, and Frank James's memory was not as good as it used to be. He never was able to find all the caches.

Cole Younger. *Library of Congress.*

Outlaw Cole Younger was eventually released from prison and was said to have come to the Fletcher area to look for James Gang treasures. Younger died at Lee's Summit, Missouri, on March 21, 1916. Frank James left his Oklahoma farm in about 1914 and died in 1915 at seventy-two years of age at the James family farm in Missouri. His niece came to the Keechi Hills area looking for the James Gang's buried caches until 1932.

Neighbors of Frank James called Addams, Pierson and Dr. Wilbur Knee watched James and Cole Younger hunt for treasure. They also searched independently and found the bones of a burro and also a burro shoe at the base of a cottonwood tree stump. They gave up without finding anything.

Deputy Sheriff Joseph Hunter of Rush Springs, Oklahoma, took up the search for James Gang treasure in 1932. An elderly man called "Cook" who had been a friend of Joseph Hunter's father appeared and gave Joseph Hunter two old cowhide maps and one sheepskin map to James Gang treasures. "Cook" was likely an associate or member of the James Gang who was about to die. Hunter never saw him again. For weeks, Hunter combed the area. He located a key mound of rocks, which he used to find another buried map. He made more than forty trips to the Keechi Hills before finding the first treasure cache. Hunter also found a prospector pick and the charred remains of eighteen burro saddles.

At a knoll north of Buzzard Roost near the foot of the north slope of Tarbone Mountain, Hunter found a buried cache about fifty yards from a rotted cottonwood tree stump. He uncovered an iron tea kettle in the ground. Inside, Hunter recovered $5,000 in gold coins ($64,000 by another account), two pearl brooches, a ruby in a gold locket, an 1811 French five-franc coin, an 1841 U.S. penny and a gold and silver pocket watch. Hunter thought this was the personal treasure of one of the James Gang outlaws.

After about two more years of searching, Hunter found a brass bucket with the words "On this 5 day of March, 1876, we whose names are scratched on thisheer bucket do bear witness one to the other." It looked like a grave, cross, burro-pack, burro shoe and arrow were etched on the bucket. Not all the words and figures on the bucket were legible. Hunter said in 1948 that he found all his treasure based on old maps. He said one map was on a cowhide and another was on the leather tongue of a boot. Joseph Hunter died in 1953 without finding the $2 million James Gang treasure. Some copies of these maps are in Steve Wilson's *Oklahoma Treasure Lost and Found* and *Rebel Gold*. There is a Jesse James Visitor Center in Cement regarding outlaws in this area.

Lost Cave with an Iron Door

Several legends indicate early Spaniards cached gold ingots and coins in a cave with an iron door. There was supposed to be a giant jail key to lock and unlock the door protecting $11 million in gold in baskets. The area north of Treasure Lake near Mount Pinchot in the Charon's Garden Wilderness Area in the Wichita Mountains Wildlife Refuge was often mentioned as its location. Others believe it could be west of Treasure Lake and Post Oak Lake, both of which were constructed with dams in the 1930s. One version of this story had Indian slaves left behind to guard the treasure. The Comanche Indians have a story that it was once a Spanish mine and they drove the Spanish from the area. In Spanish Cave, the skeleton of a Spanish soldier with Spanish objects was found in what many think was in the area of the cave with the iron door.

In the 1850s, a group of treasure hunters used a silk map and supposedly found the cave. Inside the cave were stacked gold bars, along with baskets overflowing with gold coins. Human skeletons were on the floor. A guard outside the cave warned everyone inside that there was a cloud of dust from approaching Indians. The treasure hunters quickly mounted their horses and fled to a defensible position. The Indians then blocked the cave with rocks. The treasure hunters decided to leave and return later when the Indians were not hostile. The Indians remained hostile, and the Civil War began. These treasure hunters were unable to return. This version of the story does not adequately explain how they got through the iron door.

In the early 1900s (1938 in one version), a man and his son were riding to Indiahoma from the wildlife refuge headquarters and took a shortcut through the mountains. They split from the main road and went through hills near Elk Mountain. Along the way, they saw a rusty door in a cliff in a remote canyon. Since it was almost dark, the two didn't pause to investigate. They reached their friends in Indiahoma and told them about the iron door. Their friends related the tale of the lost treasure cave with an iron door. The entire group went out the next day to search for the cave but could not find

Wichita Mountains from Mount Scott. *Author's photo.*

it. The father and son couldn't agree on where they saw the cave with an iron door. They spent many weeks looking for the iron door, without success. Some people suggest it was an old gunpowder storage cave left by miners from the Wichita Mountains gold rush.

A boy called Prince traveled with a girl and another couple in about 1910 on a trip in the Wichita Mountains. They all reportedly saw an iron door with padlocks in the side of a cliff north of Treasure Lake. Prince and the party did not investigate the door at the time. They later learned about the lost treasure cave with an iron door. Prince and his brother from Indiahoma looked for it several times, but like everyone else, they never found it.

Another father and son were hiking west of Elk Mountain and split to go different routes along the north and south rim of a canyon. The son on the south rim carried his coat, as it was a warm day. A wind gust blew his coat into the canyon, so he went to retrieve it. While in the canyon, he noticed an iron safe with a big iron lock on it. He rejoined his dad, but they were unable to find it.

Still another story has hunters in a canyon after midnight when they stumbled into an iron door in the side of the canyon with a lock they could not open. The hunters left to get tools to open the iron door but never could relocate it.

Prospector Silas Lee Ison told a story to Steve Wilson that in about 1908, a woman named Holt, who was about seventy years old, came from Missouri and stayed with him and his father for two weeks to about a month. The woman was looking for a cave with an iron door. She had a map and a very old large key to open the lock on the iron door. Lee Ison was an old prospector who for decades looked for gold in the Wichita Mountains but never found any. Another version of this story was that a lady with a large iron key came to the area between 1900 and 1905 looking for the cave with an iron door so she could use her key to open it. Ison was said to have thought it was just a loose iron safe in the canyon without a cave.

Still another account claimed the iron door in the cave was set by Belle Starr and her outlaw band to protect their loot in the mid-1880s. This story claimed Starr and a gang robbed a train heading for the Denver mint with a cargo of gold. The robbers got more than $500,000 in gold and took an iron door from the train. They went to the Wichita Mountains and put the gold in the cave with the entrance blocked by the iron door. This seems to be a pretty farfetched story on many levels, including Belle Starr's involvement.

Mexican Cache Creek Gold

Mexicans were said to have cached gold on Cache Creek south of Geronimo.

Mexican Pack Train Treasure

See Cotton County.

Mount Roosevelt Loot

Outlaw loot worth $20,000 was rumored to have been hidden on Mount Roosevelt in the Wichita Mountains Wildlife Refuge.

Mount Scott Treasure

A legend indicated Spanish treasure was hidden on Mount Scott in the Wichita Mountains Wildlife Refuge. Mount Scott is 2,464 feet high and

View from Mount Scott. *Author's photo.*

towers over the other mountains. A version of this tale states it was a Mexican treasure worth $90,000. Mount Scott has a winding road to its peak and has a lot of traffic.

Nine Carts of Treasure

J. Frank Dobie's book *Coronado's Children* has a story he got from the Comanche County surveyor in Lawton. A man with a map came to Lawton in 1905 looking for seven springs. The surveyor helped him look for the key details on the map. The hidden treasure consisted of nine carts of gold and silver. The site on the map appeared to be a place called Seven Springs on the old Fort Sill Road between Cache Creek and Beaver Creek, about thirty miles northwest of Duncan's Store. The surveyor thought the location was at Charlie Thomas's Place, as he knew there were four springs there and could be another three springs he didn't know about. After searching for a while, the man returned to Kansas. Several years later, another man came to the area and desperately wanted to farm Charlie Thomas's Place. Charlie Thomas eventually fenced off an area to sharecrop with the man. The sharecropper farmed it for three to four seasons. He was often seen systematically poking an iron rod into the soil over the land. One day, the sharecropper disappeared and left behind his shack with its contents, his team of horses, a wagon and the crop that was ready to harvest. Some speculated that he found the treasure he was looking for.

Outlaw Cache

After robbing a Kansas bank, the outlaws fled to the Wichita Mountains area while heading for the Red River. In the Wichita Mountains, Indians attacked the outlaws. The outlaws were supposed to have buried their loot about two miles south and four miles west of Geronimo. Two of them were killed, and the other died later in a Dallas, Texas hospital. Before the outlaw in Dallas died, he told a nurse attending him about the cache and gave directions to it. The nurse led a party of people to look for the loot but never found it.

In an October 18, 1907 edition of the *Lawton News-Republican*, an article said T.C. Moore and Bill F. Moore found a gun sticking up out of the ground near the Big Pasture Quarry. Digging at the site, they found a human skeleton, a buffalo rifle, a Winchester rifle, spent and unfired bullets and a saddle with the name A.E. Kelly lettered on it. In 1910, another skeleton was found on an eroding creek four miles from where the nurse and her Texas group had searched for the treasure. This site was about six miles south and three miles west of Geronimo. This second skeleton was north of where the first skeleton was found in 1907. A man digging postholes was reported to have uncovered a gallon bucket, which was taken to a Lawton bank and opened by a committee including the employer of the digger. Its contents were never made public, but it was said not to have been treasure.

Outlaw Loot

Outlaws were supposed to have buried $60,000 in gold coins in the Indiahoma area.

Rattlesnake Cave Treasure

Rattlesnake Cave in the Wichita Mountains reportedly contained gold.

Meers Store. *Oklahoma Historical Society*.

Spanish Treasure

A legend said that a Spanish treasure worth $785,000 in gold bars was hidden in Hobbs Canyon west of Meers.

Spanish Wichita Mountains Treasure

In the Wichita Mountains near Lawton, another Spanish treasure was rumored to have been cached.

See Kiowa County, "Snyder Area Treasures."

Treasure Lake

Treasure Lake was where a legend indicated that in the late 1700s, Indians attacked a Spanish mule train with gold bullion. The Spaniards threw the gold into what is now called Treasure Lake. However, the dam that holds water in Treasure Lake was not constructed until the 1930s as part of the Civilian Conservation Corps construction projects during the Great

Depression. Also, a one-hundred-pound gold calf was said to have been hidden in a Catholic priest's grave near Treasure Lake. One mile southwest of Treasure Lake in the Wichita Mountains Wildlife Refuge, a Spanish treasure cave was also rumored to be located. This treasure cave could be the same legend as the "Lost Cave with an Iron Door."

Twin Mountains Treasures

J. Frank Dobie's book *Coronado's Children* presented a story about an old Indian woman (105 years old) who came to the Twin Mountains area. She claimed a Spanish pack train with gold ore left Devil's Canyon and was ambushed by Indians. All the Spaniards were killed in the attack. The old Indian said she and two other Indians captured three burros loaded with gold ore and hid the gold ore at the foot of Twin Mountains (Twin Mountain) in the western Wichita Mountains. The location could be near Centerville. Twin Mountains are northwest of Snyder. Another tale said a Mexican found a cave with a vein of gold on the west side of the Wichita Mountains in the Twin Mountains area. This could be Kiowa County.

Also, a government payroll was said to have been hidden near the Twin Mountains. This could be a version of the Kiowa County "Camp Radzimiski Treasure" tale of lost government money.

Wildhorse Canyon Outlaw Treasure

An outlaw treasure consisting of $60,000 in gold coins may be hidden in Wildhorse Canyon, Wichita Mountains. Wildhorse Canyon is about ten miles east of Twin Mountains.

COTTON COUNTY

Mexican Pack Train Treasure

A Mexican seven-mule pack train with treasure was rumored to have been hidden about fifteen miles south of Lawton near Pecan School on Cache Creek. Indians attacked the Mexicans, and many did not survive. A Mexican survivor of the attack returned to the area in 1919 but could not find the treasure.

Spanish Gold

Spanish gold was said to have been hidden two miles west of Walters, close to Elm Springs Creek on the Williams Farm. The Spaniards were attacked with all but one killed and their wagons burned. A Mexican with a map to the treasure came to the Williams Farm many years later. Williams took the Mexican to Barefoot Spring (Elm Springs). They dug and found a large rock with several triangles but did not find any gold.

CREEK COUNTY

Bill's $60,000 Gold Cache

A Creek man called Bill had an eighty-acre allotment around 1880 about six miles southwest of Sapulpa, near Kellyville, with a creek and a bridge on the property. Bill was rich, as he sold his lands and slaves in the Southeast before migrating in the Trail of Tears to the Creek Nation. His family said he had about $60,000 in gold buried near his home. During the summer of 1880, three outlaws stopped at Bill's house and demanded his money. He refused to show them where his cache was. After some discussion, they murdered him and left. His aged daughter later returned to the area in the 1950s to search for her family's treasure but was unsuccessful in finding it. Tom Vance looked for this treasure and wrote about it in an article, "Search for the $60,000 Indian Gold Cache," in *Treasure* magazine.

Outlaw Hideouts

The Dalton Gang had a hideout that was a cave on Salt Creek about three miles southwest of Keystone, and they may have hidden some loot in or near the cave. The original town of Keystone is now under Keystone Lake, but the new town of Keystone is located southwest of the original town site. Another Dalton hideout was south of Mannford on the Berryhill Farm.

CUSTER COUNTY

Mexican Gold

While traveling from California toward St. Louis with reportedly $50,000 in gold coins, a Mexican man and his son were attacked by Comanches. The father was killed, and the son was badly wounded. The son managed to bury the gold before fleeing. In 1879, the injured Mexican boy was treated by a U.S. Army surgeon in San Antonio, Texas. The Mexican boy had a map and told the surgeon about the lost gold.

Years later, the surgeon's son traveled from Philadelphia to Corn with the treasure map. He met James (Henry) Kendall there at Kendall's store. Kendall's store had a post office and was one of the original buildings in Corn (called Korn then) in 1896. The man showed Kendall the map and told him the treasure tale. Kendall recalled that the map showed a small canyon going to the Washita River about seven miles north of present Clinton. The man searched for the gold but left after finding nothing.

Kendall passed the story to a man called Menno Dueckson, who found a canyon that fit the map. E.D. Walters hired a medium who roamed the canyon looking for clues. The medium always stopped at a central location in the canyon. Walters told Dueckson where the medium stopped. There, Dueckson dug six feet down looking for the treasure. He reportedly found a skeleton that appeared to have been Spanish, due to the material associated with it, but did not find any gold.

Soldier Treasure

A group of Armstrong Custer's cavalry reportedly gambled at a camp near Panther Creek not far from present Clinton. One man won all the money. The money was hidden near an old oak tree that had one side without limbs. A map was made, and the soldiers continued on their mission. When the man returned, he could not find the tree, as the roads had changed. One story was that it was later found. This could be in Washita County.

DELAWARE COUNTY

Ed Lockhart Loot

See Tulsa County.

Garden Cache

See Mayes County.

Lacy Mouse's Treasure

When he was forced to leave his homeland in the Southeast for Indian Territory during the Trail of Tears, full-blood Cherokee Lacy Mouse sold his North Carolina plantation and slaves. Lacy Mouse had a large sum of money when he settled near present Kenwood in the Spavinaw Hills in Delaware County or Mayes County, where he built a cabin and was prosperous.

In 1864 during the Civil War, a gang of robbers broke into Lacy Mouse's home. The robbers threatened to kill him unless he gave up his gold. The robbers grew angry, shot him through the heart and left his body in the cabin. A distant relative was in another room in the cabin when the robbers broke in. Lacy Mouse's relative overheard everything but stayed hidden, fearing for his life. The identity of the murderers remained unknown. After Lacy Mouse's death, his relatives searched in vain for his treasure. Robert F. Turpin wrote about this treasure in his magazine *Treasure Hunt*.

In the 1930s, a group of men from Missouri searched for Mouse's treasure but reportedly found nothing. In 1943, a farmhand was plowing what had been the Lacy Mouse Farm when, just before sundown, he saw reflections from several objects in the middle of the field. Upon walking over to the reflections, he found several gold coins and the remains of an old leather sack. The farmhand returned the next day with a shovel but was unable to locate any more coins. It was thought these coins were from Lacy Mouse's cache and there could be more nearby. This was before there were metal detectors to find such treasure.

Lost Gold Mines

East of Spavinaw Lake, in Delaware County or Mayes County, a number of lost gold mines were reportedly located. Indians, Spaniards and Mormons supposedly mined there. Gold ingots were said to have been stacked inside one mine when outlaws chased the miners from the area. There is a granite outcrop downstream of the Spavinaw Dam, but most of the rock in the area is sedimentary rock, which does not contain gold. W.C. Jameson's *Lost Mines and Buried Treasure of Oklahoma* discusses the Lost Mormon Mine, which some claimed was under Spavinaw Lake. Other minerals besides gold are possibly in this area.

Mexican Miner Treasure

In about 1850, Mexicans came to the Cherokee Nation looking for markers on the Grand River and Elk River in the Cowskin Prairie, Delaware County and Ottawa County area. They had a sheepskin map with them. It is not known if they found any treasure.

Perdue's Treasure

A man named Perdue buried $500 near his home, which may have been near Spavinaw. He was killed during the Civil War, and no one has found his cache.

Wooster McCoy's Cache

See Mayes County.

DEWEY COUNTY

Riley Ranch Hideout

"Big Jim" Riley's Ranch near Taloga, on the South Canadian River, was another hideout for the Doolin-Dalton Gang. Riley was a teamster with a

Cheyenne wife and a ranch far from roads and towns. The Doolin-Dalton Gang planned the Wharton (now Perry) train robbery from Riley's Ranch in May 1891. After the robbery, they divided up the loot at Riley's Ranch. Riley's Ranch was also where the Doolin-Dalton Gang divided up the loot from the 1892 robbery of the Red Rock train. Although no treasure story is associated with this ranch, some loot could have been hidden in the area by the individual outlaws.

Spanish Gold Coins Found

West of Vici, several burro loads of Spanish gold were supposed to have been cached in a canyon. In 1926, Walter Smith related this story. A number of human skulls were found in the area. Legend had it that Indians attacked and killed all the Spaniards. Some Spanish coins were found in a canyon in 1912 near Vici, which gives some validity to this tale.

ELLIS COUNTY

Diego Parilla Treasure

Spaniard Colonel Diego Ortiz Parilla was said to have buried a treasure on Wolf Creek. Parilla led several Spanish expeditions, including one in 1759 against Comanches and Tuovayas on the Red River in the Spanish Fort, Texas area.

GARVIN COUNTY

Eight Mile Creek Treasure

Twenty mule loads of Spanish gold (or silver) were said to have been buried near Eight Mile Creek. Another version of this story was that $2.5 million in gold bars was hidden not far from Davis on Eight Mile Creek. It may be in Murray County.

Fort Arbuckle Treasure

Fort Arbuckle was established in 1852 on the California Trail on Wild Horse Creek about a quarter mile north of Hoover. The United States abandoned Fort Arbuckle before the Civil War, so Confederate troops were stationed there. A U.S. Army payroll with gold coins (gold and silver coins) from Fort Leavenworth, Kansas, bound for Fort Arbuckle in 1868 or 1869 was reportedly ambushed by outlaws near Mill Creek. Maybe five outlaws were killed in the attack, along with all the soldiers. One version claimed the payroll was buried in three locations by the surviving outlaws. The outlaws parted, with one later being captured. The other surviving outlaw (or several outlaws) headed for Mexico.

In the 1890s, a dying ex-convict in St. Joseph, Missouri, was supposed to have taken refuge in a livery stable and told the good Samaritan working there about the robbery. A friend of the livery stable worker told Samuel H. Davis about the tale. Davis was the businessman for whom the town of Davis, Oklahoma, was named. Davis spent much time looking for the treasure without finding it. It was said to have been hidden near Davis in Murray County, possibly in a cave. A group of five Mexicans appeared

Fort Arbuckle. *Oklahoma Historical Society*.

on Mill Creek searching for something. The landowner reported finding a rusted iron pot in a deep hole with imprints of coins in the pot. One treasure hunter thought the treasure was buried on Guy Sandy Creek and is now under the Lake of the Arbuckles.

GRADY COUNTY

Found Cache

In 1938, Floyd Terril found a cache of $38,650, with much of it in gold coins, near Chickasha. Many people thought was part of the James Gang treasures.

Tuttle Cache

A cache was said to be hidden east of Tuttle in three graves. Some trees had been marked in the area to identify the treasure location. This may have been a James Gang treasure.

GRANT COUNTY

Found Chisholm Trail Gold

A man known by the initials G.A.Y. heard his grandfather tell a story about being the trail foreman for a rancher who drove 1,200 head of cattle up the Chisholm Trail from Texas to Newton, Kansas. The rancher paid off the drovers and his foreman and headed back to Texas with $3,600 from the cattle sale. The foreman left a day behind the rancher. The foreman found his boss's body on the Chisholm Trail about a mile north of Sewell's Stockade. Sewell's Stockade was built in the 1870s as protection against Indian attack. It was about a mile north of the Salt Fork of the Arkansas River, on the trail where the Osage Blackdog Trail forded the river. The rancher had been scalped, but since he still had money in his pocket, the foreman did not think outlaws killed him. The foreman knew that his money had been wrapped in a slicker and tied to his boss's saddle when he left Kansas.

In the summer of 1965, G.A.Y. decided to look for the treasure. His theory was that the rancher hid the money before going to Sewell's Stockade and was on the way back to retrieve it when he was ambushed and murdered by Indians. G.A.Y. found Sewell's Stockade to be a half mile south of Jefferson. He spent a week looking over the Chisholm Trail trying to figure out where the rancher hid his money. At one location, his metal detector got a strong signal. He dug in a rock-filled hole. He found a rotting slicker and leather bag with $3,600 in old gold coins about a foot below ground level. This story was detailed as "Chisholm Trail Treasure" in the *Artifact* magazine in 1966, written by C.H. McKennon and G.A.Y.

GREER COUNTY

King Mountain Treasure

A legend indicated that Spanish or Mexican miners buried treasure on the west side of 2,411-foot-high King Mountain. The miners were attacked by Indians and retreated to the top of the mountain to try to fight off the Indians. Part of King Mountain is located in Quartz Mountain State Park. This treasure may have been found and recovered.

Lugert-Area Treasures

In the Lugert area, Spanish gold coins were supposed to have been hidden in the Wichita Mountains. A lost Spanish mine was also reportedly near Lugert.

HARMON COUNTY

Winchester Gang Treasure

The Winchester Gang may have cached their loot of gold coins north of Hollis near the Texas line or between Hollis and the Red River.

HASKELL COUNTY

Belle Starr Treasures

Belle Starr was born as Myra Maybelle Shirley and was called the Bandit Queen. She had a very colorful life hanging around outlaws and being an outlaw herself. During the Civil War, her family associated with Quantrill's guerrillas, including the James brothers and the Younger brothers. Her first husband, James W. "Jim" Reed, was an ex-Quantrill guerrilla member and outlaw who later was killed in Paris, Texas. She married Cherokee outlaw Sam Starr in 1880. In 1882, Sam and Belle were convicted of horse stealing and served nine months each in a federal Detroit, Michigan prison. Sam Starr was shot in a gunfight with policeman Frank West in Whitefield in December 1886 and died the next day. Belle Starr next married Jim July Starr in order to remain in the Cherokee Nation.

Belle Starr reportedly hid treasure near her place at Younger's Bend, an isolated ranch north of the Canadian River four miles west of Briartown. The most likely tale is that a Cherokee named Big Head buried $10,000 in gold coins near the cabin at Younger's Bend, which had been originally

Belle Starr's house at Younger's Bend. *Oklahoma Historical Society.*

Left: Belle Starr's grave. *Oklahoma Historical Society*.

Right: Belle Starr, the Outlaw Queen. *Wikipedia*.

constructed by Dempsey Hannel. Big Head died, and people wondered where his money was hidden. Belle and Sam Starr took over the cabin and hunted for Big Head's gold. Lots of holes were dug without finding the treasure.

Belle Starr supposedly buried treasure in several places in Oklahoma, including in the Wichita Mountains. (See Comanche County, "Lost Cave with an Iron Door.") Robbers Cave in Latimer County has also been mentioned as a Belle Starr treasure site. Both are extremely unlikely. A Belle Starr hideout at Inola Hill near Inola, Rogers County, reportedly once had a rock tower on top of it as a sentry post, marking another area of her escapades.

Belle Starr was riding between Fort Smith and Younger's Bend when she was ambushed on February 3, 1889, and killed by several shotgun blasts. She was forty. Edgar A. Watson was likely to have killed her, as he formerly sharecropped part of her land and there was bad blood between them. Legend has it that Watson was picking up a letter for her about the location of a treasure and wanted her out of the way so he could recover it. Belle Starr's son Eddie Reed was also a suspect in her murder, as she had recently beaten him over a horse. Belle Starr was buried at Younger's Bend on Belle Starr Creek, about four miles west of Briartown. Her grave was disturbed in 1890 by someone after her expensive pistol and jewelry.

Dr. John J. Hayes's Lost Gold

Dr. John J. Hayes had a trading post, boat landing and warehouse called Canadian or Canadian Shoals on the Arkansas River where the California Road crossed the Arkansas River. It was at a crossing about one mile above the confluence of the Canadian and Arkansas Rivers. Before the Civil War, Dr. Hayes grew rich from trading with travelers, Cherokees and Choctaws. Steamers and boats between Fort Gibson, Cherokee Nation, and Fort Smith, Arkansas, stopped at his boat landing to pick up and drop off cargo.

Dr. Hayes was a Confederate. When Union forces took over Fort Gibson and Fort Smith, he fled to Confederate Chickasaw Nation refugee camps after burying $15,000 to $20,000 in gold near his home. In those violent times, Dr. Hayes was afraid he would be robbed if he tried to take his life savings with him when he fled the area.

Surviving Confederate refugees in the Indian nations did not quickly return to their homes after the Civil War ended due to Union Indian hostility. In 1866, Dr. Hayes and a friend returned to his home site to recover his treasure. There was still a lot of hatred and revenge killings going on from Civil War atrocities. Pro-Union Cherokee Indians, known as Pins, followed Dr. Hayes and his friend after they left the Chickasaw Nation and entered Cherokee lands. The Pins wore pins on their lapels to signify membership in the secret and antislavery pro–United States Keetoowah Society. Dr. Hayes and his friend feared they would be murdered if they dug up his gold then. They returned to the Chickasaw Nation, intending to secretly return in the fall to recover the gold. Before they could do so, Dr. Hayes died of a sudden illness. His gold likely still remains hidden somewhere near Canadian Shoals in Haskell County or Muskogee County.

HUGHES COUNTY

Fish Creek Gold

Gold bars and coins may have been hidden on Fish Creek.

Warren Mun's Strongbox of Gold

During the Civil War, Union soldiers destroyed Warren Mun's house and lands in the Southeast. After losing almost everything, he headed west to start over. Mun gathered his wife and daughter in a mule-drawn wagon with a few household goods and what was left of his life savings in twenty-dollar gold pieces.

They entered the Indian nations at Fort Smith, Arkansas, and drove west on the California Road. They crossed the north–south Texas Road near present McAlester, Oklahoma. He and his family set up camp one night at the edge of a small canyon just north of the South Canadian River near present Holdenville. A party of Indians stopped by his camp but soon left. Mun grew frightened, as he feared they would return to rob him. He quickly put his gold in a strongbox and buried it near this camp in a cavern beside a dripping spring. His daughter later said that the box was too heavy for her to pick up.

Since they were camped near a busy road, more strangers later came to their camp that night. Mun decided not to risk revealing his cache. Warren Mun and his family headed west the next morning with the strangers. They left their gold behind, intending to come back soon and get it, but they traveled too far west to return to retrieve the gold. They continued to California and started a new life. Warren Mun never made it back to get his treasure. His daughter returned to Oklahoma to search for the gold many years after her father and mother had died, but she was unable to find the treasure. She told local residents about it and then returned to California.

Local landowners have hunted for the gold along with many people with metal detectors. The strongbox was hidden halfway between Camp Holmes and the junction of the Texas Road and California Road. Dripping springs are located in the area along with canyons nearby. Hugh Zachary wrote an article in *True Treasure* titled "Oklahoma's Cache of Southern Gold" about his search for this treasure. There are no reports of this gold ever being found, so it is probably near some dried-up spring near the California Road, which was several parallel trails, not normally just one road. There are likely dripping springs in the area after big rains if they have not been plowed over.

JACKSON COUNTY

Eldorado's Lost Gold

Several lost gold stories are associated with the small community of Eldorado. One legend suggested a Spanish burro train with gold was ambushed in the area and the gold was cached nearby. Another story was that two wagons with eight men, women and children were returning east after successfully finding gold in California. The miners had more than $60,000 worth of gold, which would have been more than two hundred pounds (worth more than $5 million today). The wagons were attacked by Indians near Greta, which is about five miles northwest of Eldorado. The gold was buried. A man and a little girl escaped, and the rest were killed. The two headed east and were rescued by a couple of cowboys at what became known as Wanderers Creek. The man returned about thirty years later to look for the buried gold, but everything had changed. He had no markers. He worked as a sheepherder in the area as he looked for the gold, but he never found it.

George Reeves and Ernest Dameron looked for the gold for years. Reeves found markers in the 1920s and 1930s and found a cave with buckles and other items inside. The rumor was that he also found a gold/brass crucifix. Ernest Dameron, who lived a couple of miles from Reeves, also looked for treasure in the area. There were several indications that something had happened near Eldorado based on material that has been found over the years. No gold finds have been reported. Bob Turpin wrote an article on these called "Find Buried Treasure in Oklahoma" for *Treasure* magazine, which was a reprint of "Eldorado's Spanish Gold" in his *Treasure Hunt* magazine.

JEFFERSON COUNTY

Addington Treasure

What is called the Addington Treasure was another likely outlaw cache discussed in the Warren Getler and Bob Brewer book *Rebel Gold*. The Addington Treasure site is on the Chisholm Trail near Monument Hill, which is a few miles east of Addington. The *Daily Oklahoman* reported in an interview with Michael Griffith and his family in 1995 that they found treasure in eastern Oklahoma near Poteau. Bob Brewer used one of the copies of Joseph Hunter's Jesse James maps, which he called the Wolf Map, and went to where he thought the treasure was buried. Brewer found a freshly dug hole and was convinced Michael Griffith had found the treasure.

See Comanche County, "James Gang $2 Million Cache and Other Caches."

Spanish Treasure Reported Found

An 1884 article in the *Fort Worth Gazette* claimed a brass cannon, pack saddles, swords, armor, old manuscripts, gold crosses and $25,000 worth of gold and silver coins and ingots were found in a cave two miles upriver from Spanish Fort on the Oklahoma side of the Red River. The reporter interviewed people in a saloon who claimed that five men with dogs were chasing panthers when a panther ran into the small cave in a bluff. One of these hunters bravely crawled in the cave after the panther and discovered the Spanish treasure. The site of this treasure cave could have been on the south side of the Red River. The Red River has changed its location many times over the years. This story is questionable, as fictional stories were often reported in newspapers and presented as the truth. The reporter never saw any treasure, and there does not appear to have been a follow-up story.

JOHNSON COUNTY

Bill Cook's Lost Loot

Bill Cook was the leader of the Cook Gang, which committed robberies in Indian Territory and Oklahoma Territory. The lost loot Bill Cook was known for was the result of a four-man robbery at a water stop northeast of Ardmore, Carter County. In October 1894 (probably a bad date), Bill Cook and his gang climbed onboard a Rock Island Pacific train. Cook and one outlaw robbed the passengers of money and jewelry while one outlaw kept the train engineer and fireman under control and another outlaw robbed the mail car. They were said to have stolen $62,000 from the safe alone, which included gold and silver coins.

The outlaws fled south and east with a posse after them. They went through Springtown, and north of Tishomingo, they crossed the Little Blue River. They stopped at Delaware Creek, where Cook's companions wanted to split up the loot and head off in different directions. There was reportedly a heated discussion over the splits, and Cook supposedly killed all three men. With all the loot, he dug a hole and cached the money. The posse was nearby and caught up with him. He got a bullet through his shoulder. Cook fell off his horse and was later found by Charley Barnett, who took him to a doctor in Tupelo. In gratitude, Bill Cook told him about the treasure and said that he could have it, as Cook thought he was dying. However, he recovered enough to leave Tupelo before he could be arrested and jailed.

In researching this story, a number of sources indicate that Bill Cook and his gang robbed a number of people on the road between Fort Gibson and Vinita in late October 1894. On October 22, 1894, Cook and three outlaws tried to rob the Arkansas Flyer in Wagoner by throwing the switch to push it onto a siding, but it did not work. The train did not stop but continued down the tracks, so they got no money from that attempted robbery. They robbed the Fort Gibson train depot. People in the area felt defenseless. The Muskogee Indian agent wired for military troops to protect the population. In the gang were Cherokee Bill and the Verdigris Kid. The gang split up, and the law chased them.

Bill Cook's luck ran out in Fort Sumner, New Mexico Territory, where he was arrested on January 11, 1895. He was taken to Fort Smith, Arkansas, where he was tried by Judge Isaac Parker, the hanging judge, and convicted on twelve counts of robbery. Cook was sent to federal prison in Albany, New York, to serve a forty-five-year sentence, and he died in prison.

Barnett was thrilled to learn of Bill Cook's death. Barnett had been afraid Cook might kill him over knowing where Cook's treasure was cached. Barnett told a federal marshal about the cached loot, but the marshal did not seem to have recovered it.

Writer, trader and rancher Maurice Kildare (penname for Gladwell Toney Richardson) learned of the treasure story and talked to Charley Barnett, who told him the directions he remembered. Kildare's family had a ranch in Oklahoma nearby. Kildare wrote a lot of western articles, including a number for treasure hunting magazines. He and five other people spent a lot of time searching the area between Bromide and Clarita near Delaware Creek. This treasure site could be in Johnson County, Coal County or Atoka County. Charley Plummer showed them a shaft covered by a trapdoor. At the bottom of the shaft, two ten-dollar gold pieces, four silver dollars, several quarters and dimes were recovered. Some were dated 1878. They later found buried skeletons, which might have been those of the gang members Bill Cook was said to have killed. Flooding likely removed markers to the site near Delaware Creek. The loot was thought to have been hidden on the McMillian property, which later became the Dotson farm. This is one of those outlaw loot stories that has a lot of holes in it but also has some potential to have lost treasure. It is not far from the Wapanucka Treasures, discussed following.

Found Old Mine

In 1912, about fifteen miles from Bromide, some Missouri, Oklahoma and Gulf Railroad employees found an old mine based on an elderly Indian's directions. It may have been Spanish or French, for it was old. An ore sample was said to have assayed two hundred ounces of silver per ton and 63 percent lead. The mine, however, was not economic and was abandoned.

Wapanucka Treasures

The Warren Getler and Bob Brewer book *Rebel Gold* documents several small treasures found northwest of Wapanucka, Johnson County, not far from Wapanucka Academy, which is on a high ridge above Delaware Creek. Wapanucka Academy was also called Rock Academy and is now in ruins. It was established in 1852 as a boarding school for Chickasaw girls. During the Civil War, it was a Confederate headquarters, hospital and prison. After the Civil War, the Chickasaw Nation operated it as a school until it was sold in 1911. There was a cemetery west of the buildings that contained the 1857 grave of teacher Mary C. Greenleaf.

These likely outlaw caches were found mostly due to map interpretation by Bob Brewer and Michael Griffith. It looks as if these small caches were made by outlaws to recover when they needed funds while in hiding or were on the run. *Rebel Gold*'s premise is that Jesse James and others were members of the Knights of the Golden Circle and were putting treasure away for a future revival of the Confederacy (the Lost Cause). Lee James Hawk and Del Schrader's book *Jesse James Was One of His Names* is an interesting work on potential Knights of the Golden Circle activities. See chapter 4 on the Knights of the Golden Circle.

In about 1994, the first cache found near Wapanucka was in a glass jar with less than $100 in face value of coins dated from 1812 to 1880. It was located based on triangulation of symbols and a buried gun pointing to the

Wapanucka Academy. *Oklahoma Historical Society*.

cache. It was buried about a foot deep. The cache was mostly Morgan silver dollars with some gold coins. *Rebel Gold* said it was about one and a half miles west of Wapanucka Academy.

A second small cache was found by Michael Griffith and his family without Bob Brewer, which caused considerable conflict. This second treasure was less than $100 in face value of silver and gold coins dated from the 1830s to 1880 that were buried in a ceramic spittoon near a tree. This was found using a copy of a reputed Jesse James map with key markers locating the treasure. The treasure finders did not get approval from the property owners (but did from a party who rented the property to run cattle), which caused more conflict and controversy. A large Knights of the Golden Circle treasure ($200,000 face value) was thought by Brewer and Griffith to be in the area based on a map. Griffith reportedly told Bob Brewer he recovered $2,200 at the Wapanucka site based on the map. Bob Brewer in *Rebel Gold* thought much of the money recovered was at the Jefferson County, Addington Treasure site. The Wapanucka site was owned by the Galbraith sisters of Tulsa. Markings of "JJ" (maybe Jesse James), "11,000" and a turtle were cut into a bluff that served as key markers to a Jesse James map that led to the cache's discovery. The inscriptions in the ledge have reportedly been destroyed. A treasure hunting agreement was made on this property, and the land was later sold. Nobody has reported finding any more treasure.

KAY COUNTY

Arkansas River Cache

Kit Dalton, who wrote *Under the Black Flag*, was a cousin of the famous Dalton outlaws. Kit Dalton claimed to have been a member of the James Gang when he was interviewed in 1913 in Memphis, Tennessee. He said Jesse James buried $20,000 just above the B&M Ford, about a mile south of Ponca City. Jesse James's horse and pack mule were worn out, so he buried his money at the base of a tree and fired three bullets into the tree to form a triangle on the west bank of the Arkansas River. Kit Dalton claimed he had visited the area but did not find the treasure. A newspaper article in the *Ponca City Courier* on January 22, 1913, is the source of this story.

California Miners' Treasure

In 1853, a group of returning California gold miners (likely Virginians) buried several iron cooking pots of gold on the Arkansas River bank near the Black Dog Trail Crossing (Black Dog Crossing). This treasure was reputed to be buried north of the crossing along Wolf Creek at the first of two ravines called Happy Hollow and Lime Hollow about eight miles east of Newkirk or north of Newkirk. Osage Indians attacked the miners, who hid their gold. A broken rifle was put in two forks of a tree as a marker. One wounded miner made it back to Virginia. Before the survivor died, he gave instructions to his family on how to find the treasure. A search party came to look for the gold but never found it. A piece of limestone was found in a tree fork, which some thought may have replaced the broken rifle. So far, no one has reported finding any gold.

KINGFISHER COUNTY

Train Robbery Loot

In 1895, an outlaw was said to have been chased by lawmen into an evangelical church religious camp meeting just outside Dover. The outlaw had robbed a train the previous night of several thousand dollars in gold. He went to the camp meeting to blend in with other strangers there. He arrived with full saddlebags. During the camp meeting, he left for the nearby woods. He returned with empty-looking saddlebags. A short time later, lawmen in the camp meeting recognized the outlaw, and a gunfight ensued. The outlaw ran to a house and escaped out the back door. He left a trail of blood but made it to his horse and rode out of Dover. A posse went after him. The outlaw was found, arrested and taken to nearby Hennessey. Someone found his horse with empty saddlebags. The outlaw died without disclosing where the stolen loot was cached. Ben Townsend related this tale in *Treasure World* magazine.

KIOWA COUNTY

Camp Radzimski Treasure

A U.S. government treasure consisting of $40,000 in a wagon was supposedly en route to pay soldiers and was ambushed near Camp Radzimski near Snyder. The treasure may have been buried near Camp Radzimski. Camp Radzimski was established in September 1858 by Captain Earl Van Dorn and the U.S. cavalry to provide protection from Indian attacks. The camp was abandoned in 1859. During the Civil War, Confederate troops were stationed there. Camp Radzimski is about 1.5 miles north and 2.5 miles west of Mountain Park. One version of this tale places the hidden treasure near Otter Creek (see "Otter Creek Loot").

Devil's Canyon Treasures

A Spanish mining village called San Bernardo was said to have been in Devil's Canyon near Flattop. A smelter was built by a nearby mine. Didaco Lopes, Friar Juan de Salas and Esteban Perea reportedly did missionary work in the Wichita Mountains area and established a Spanish mission in the area in 1611. The miners' village was attacked by Indians, with most of the miners massacred. Skeletons and old Spanish equipment have been found in the area by settlers who plowed the canyon.

A brass cannon filled with gold was supposedly hidden on the west end of Devil's Canyon below a tree with a cross carved on it. Forty or fifty burros of treasure were possibly hidden nearby in a deep cavern. Another tale said nine burro packs of Spanish gold were hidden in a cavern near the floor of Devil's Canyon.

Gold bars worth about $112,000 were rumored to be hidden in a cave in Devil's Canyon about six miles upstream from Devil's Canyon and two and a half miles west of the North Fork of the Red River. An old mine shaft with mined ore may also be in Devil's Canyon.

A legend claimed there is a treasure in a cave near Devil's Canyon. The treasure was brought by a ship sailing up the North Fork of the Red River. The cave was sealed, and the old ship's anchor was left outside the cave to mark the site. Some people have reportedly seen this anchor over the years.

The *Mangum Star* newspaper reported that in 1902, an 83 percent pure gold nugget weighing about eighty-five pounds was reportedly found at the mouth of Devil's Canyon. Most think this gold was from a possible massacre of gold miners returning from the California gold rush. Metates with gold flakes embedded in them were also reportedly said to have been discovered in the area.

Flattop Mountain Outlaw Cache

Bob Herring's outlaw cache of $31,000 was said to have been hidden in 1894 under a rock near Flattop Mountain near Devil's Canyon. The money was stolen by the Barker Gang. Herring stole it from the three other gang members, who he thought were going to kill him. After hiding the loot, he later killed the surviving gang member. Bob Herring died in the Huntsville, Texas prison. He gave a map to the treasure location to his cousin Josh Drake, but Drake and his son were never able to locate it.

Hallet's Lost Gold Mine

A legend indicated Hallet's Lost Gold Mine was on Rattlesnake Mountain.

King Mountain Treasure

Mexican miners may have buried a treasure on the western part of King Mountain. One story said the treasure was found and retrieved.

Otter Creek Loot

In 1885, a stagecoach from Henrietta, Texas, was reportedly en route to Fort Sill with $96,000 in gold coins in bags (which would weigh about three hundred pounds) when a gang of seven outlaws held up the stage just before it reached the Charley Crossing station at the Red River. The bags of gold coins were taken, and the outlaws crossed the Red River and headed north for the Wichita Mountains. A rider from the Charley Crossing station quickly rode to Henrietta, Texas, where a telegraph was sent to Fort Sill alerting the U.S. Army of the robbery. A U.S. Army cavalry detachment was sent to intercept the robbers. At Cutthroat Gap, the troopers met the outlaws and killed five. Two outlaws escaped on horseback with the loot. One outlaw was badly wounded. Since the bags of gold were heavy and the troopers would be in pursuit, the outlaws stopped at a crossing on Otter Creek, about four miles south of Cold Spring at the Lower Narrows.

The wounded outlaw died there and may have been buried at the site. The surviving outlaw supposedly cached the bags of gold on the west side of Otter Creek. He then chased the horses off to leave false trails. The outlaw fled down Otter Creek to escape. The troopers eventually found the fresh grave and went after the trails left by the horses.

In 1935, four men showed up at Cold Spring looking for a certain crossing on Otter Creek. They talked to grocer Arthur Henderson. They told him about the robbery and the map they had regarding the buried gold. The grocer told them about the Otter Creek crossing that might be what they were looking for. He thought it was on the Navajo Trail, which connected Fort Sill to Fort Elliott, Texas. Later, a number of holes were found along Otter Creek, which were likely made by the visitors. It was not known if they found what they were looking for.

Instead of outlaws, there is a version of the Cutthroat Gap story where renegade Indians were related to this tale. Otter Creek also is in Tillman County, so this tale could cover that county as well.

San Bernardo Treasure

From the mining district and village of San Bernardo, legends indicated Spaniards mined gold and silver with Indian slaves until they were attacked and run off by Indians. The Kiowa Indians may have attacked the Spanish settlement. Legends indicated Spanish mining took place in the Wichita

Mountains, although no evidence has been found of economic gold or silver being mined. The village site may be about twenty-five miles from Hobart.

The Spaniards reportedly hid gold and silver in a large trench with symbols left behind to identify the cache. This may have been when the Comanche, Tonkawa and Hasinai Indians attacked Mission Santa Cruz de San Saba, Texas, in 1758. The Spaniards in present Oklahoma were said to have all been ambushed by Indians and killed or chased out of the country. One surviving Spaniard's relatives later came to Ada, Pontotoc County, from Mexico to search for the treasure. This man returned to Mexico but left a map behind with a friend. His friend discovered several key markers he thought indicated where the treasure had been buried. The man spent a lot of effort drilling and probing for the treasure. He hit something and drilled through it. He thought it was a trench but failed to find any treasure. In the 1930s, his sons arrived with bulldozers and backhoes and a dredge line. Huge holes were dug, but no treasure was recovered. In the 1960s, another unsuccessful group hunted for the treasure. An old arrastre was reportedly found with silver slag nearby, which indicates some mining.

Snyder-Area Treasures

Several treasure stories are associated with the Snyder area besides the Otter Creek Treasure. The Lost Gold Bell Mine was supposed to be within three miles of Snyder. In a cave north of Snyder, a cache of Confederate money was reportedly discovered.

Tepee Mountain Outlaw Loot

In a Tepee Mountain cave, outlaw loot may have been cached. The cave was big enough to ride a horse into. This mountain is also known as Mount Webster. It was called Tepee Mountain due to its shape.

Twin Mountains Treasures

See Comanche County.

LATIMER COUNTY

Kunneotubby Treasure

Choctaw Kunneotubby lived on Kunneotubby Creek, north of Wilburton. He was known to have buried money somewhere. Cattle thieves murdered him. His family never found his secret cache.

Robbers Cave

A legend said robbers hid more than one hundred mule loads of gold ore in a sealed cave within a half mile of Robbers Cave State Park, which is a few miles north of Wilburton in the San Bois Mountains. Originally called Latimer State Park, Robbers Cave State Park was a former Boy Scouts of America camp acquired by the State of Oklahoma. The area has sandstone block outcrops that sometimes form overhangs or fallen blocks of sandstone that make caves. The stories of Jesse James and Belle Starr treasures are likely tourist promotional stories. Likewise, the Dalton Gang, Youngers and Rufus Buck Gang were said to have used the area as a refuge. The last time I was in the park, it had a small history exhibit on the area.

Robbers Cave. *Oklahoma Historical Society*.

San Bois Mountains Loot

Some loot might be hidden in the San Bois Mountains.

Wilburton Outlaw Caches

A Seminole outlaw called Blackface supposedly buried three sets of loot near Wilburton. A dry creek in the nearby hills was said to be where the treasure was hidden. This loot included gold bars of reportedly $11 million in value. (See Cherokee County, "Blackface Treasures," for another Blackface story.)

In a cave not far from Wilburton, an outlaw cache was reportedly concealed. Cherokee outlaws also supposedly hid three different caches of loot in the Wilburton area near a creek. They had made a number of robberies, but their career ended and they were unable to recover their loot. This could be another version of the Blackface Gang treasure.

Robert Randolph, Elmo Randolph and Tom Casey were fishing about October 27, 1905, near Wilburton when they found $400 consisting of $5, $10, $20 and $50 gold coins in a dry creek. Some had a date of 1821. This treasure was likely hidden long ago. It may have been part of the lost treasures discussed previously.

LE FLORE COUNTY

Buzzard Hill Spanish Treasure

On Buzzard Hill, Spanish gold bars and coins were supposed to have been buried north of Spiro, near Pocola or ten miles east of Spiro, according to another variation of this story. Another tale claimed a lost Spanish gold mine was in the area. This is an area of sedimentary rock, which is not gold bearing. A Mexican visited the area in the 1880s looking for treasure from tales that had been passed down to him.

$40,000 Mule Train Loot

In the Turkey Mountains, $40,000 in gold coins from a mule train attack were reportedly hidden.

Found Treasure

Michael Griffith claimed to have uncovered treasure near Poteau in a newspaper interview.

Henry Starr Treasures

Henry Starr was a Cherokee who robbed a lot of banks—mostly in Oklahoma. On March 27, 1893, he and Frank Cheney robbed the Caney Valley Bank in Caney, Kansas, of $2,000 to $2,500. Starr said it was $4,900 in bills, with no coins.

A legend said that in Le Flore County, six to seven miles east of U.S. 271 near Holsum Valley Road, a half-bushel of silver coins was buried from the Starr Gang's robberies. Newt Lloyd claimed a member of Henry Starr's gang farmed an area on the Lee Elwood Ranch. The gang left money in his care. He hid it and then refused to share with them. He fled the area, leaving the money, his wife and his kids behind. Later, his family moved to Arkansas. The wife returned but could not find the money. She told Newt Lloyd's brother about the lost money. The loot was in a cotton sack inside a half-bushel basket in a hole, which was refilled with a large rock put on top. It was buried near their cabin on a hill before it sloped into a field.

Henry Starr, 1915. *Oklahoma Historical Society*.

Jacques Tisserand wrote an article in *True Treasure* magazine that discussed searching for the treasure. He and a friend found a 1912 nickel and 1914 dime in the area, which could have been part of the treasure. It could be that the treasure had been recovered.

Other legends say Henry Starr hid $100,000 in gold coins near Rose, Mayes County. Another $135,000 Henry Starr cache was said to be in the Pryor, Mayes County area. Starr and five of his gang robbed the Missouri, Kansas and Texas

(Katy) Railroad train on May 2, 1893, at Pryor Creek. Starr claimed to have gotten $6,000 in cash and uncut diamonds from the express car and two passenger cars at the Pryor Creek robbery. On June 5, 1893, the Starr Gang robbed the People's Bank in Bentonville, Arkansas, of a reported $11,001.53 in cash, as well as gold and silver coins. Henry Starr was captured in Colorado Springs, Colorado. He later was released from prison and tried to go straight. He got into the movie production business in Tulsa, but he was short of money and returned to robbing banks. Henry Starr died in 1921 after being wounded in a Harrison, Arkansas bank robbery.

Lost Silver Dollar Cache

Choctaw Mrs. Bell told her son Buddy Bell that she hid a cache of five hundred silver dollars under a large oak tree near Summerfield. The Bell place was a mile west of the mouth of the Fourche Maline River and Holsom Creek. This cache may still remain.

Outlaw Treasure

Another outlaw cache was said to have been hidden near Wistler.

Round Mountain Lost Mine

A few miles south of Heavener near Round Mountain, the Spanish were rumored to have mined silver and hidden it close by. Round Mountain is flat on the top and is about two miles long. This is sedimentary rock, so a silver deposit is unlikely, but it could have been iron pyrite or other minerals.

Winding Stair Mountains Lost Mine

Uncle Bob Blankenship claimed he found a gold mine on the northern part of the Winding Stair Mountains at the head of Wild Horse Canyon some four to five miles north of Smithville.

LOGAN COUNTY

Guthrie Treasure Found

In 1869, a traveler buried a pot with $4,500 in gold and $500 in silver while traveling to New Mexico. His cousin later came to Guthrie and negotiated with a banker, who made a deal with the landowner in April 1895. The banker, landowner and others dug up the cache, according to a Guthrie newspaper.

Doolin-Dalton Gang Hangouts

Bill Doolin's hideouts were at the headwaters of Turkey Creek and on the Cimarron River south of Yale and in the Turkey Trak Ranch area of the Sac and Fox Indian Reservation. The H-X Bar Ranch was on Cowboy Flat (Flats), about thirteen miles northeast of Guthrie, and was owned by Oscar D. Halsell, who hired Bill Doolin as a cowboy at various times between 1882 and 1890. Dave Fitzgerald's Ranch was also about eleven to fifteen miles northeast of Guthrie and was used by the Dalton Gang and Doolin-Dalton Gang. Cowboy Flat was an area along the Cimarron River that had good grazing land. There is a possibility that some outlaws' caches could have been made in the area of these ranches.

LOVE COUNTY

Twenty Mule Loads of Gold

Twenty mule loads of Spanish gold were supposed to have been hidden near a big rock about fifty miles southwest of the Red River big bend near where the Little Washita River joins the Red River. This cache could be in present Love County or Marshall County.

Spanish Fort–Area Treasures

See Marshall County.

MAJOR COUNTY

Found Cache

A cache of more than $2,000 dating from the 1850s was found by Alfred Abrams while digging a well near Cleo Springs in 1895.

Money in a Cave

A tale from the January 15, 1903 edition of the *Daily Oklahoman* said a man entered a cave in the Glass Mountains and found old money pinned under a large rock he couldn't budge. He managed to tear off a piece of a twenty-dollar bill. The cave was said to be along the upper end of Barney Creek. Some thought this might be some of outlaw Dick Yeager's (Zip Wyatt's) lost loot.

See Blaine County, "Yeager-Black Gang Treasure."

MARSHALL COUNTY

Spanish Fort–Area Treasures

The Spanish Fort area on the Texas side of the Red River was where a big battle between Spaniards and French-allied Indians took place in 1759, which the Spanish lost. There was an old Spanish Trail from Santa Fe to New Orleans and Louisiana Territory that ran along the Red River in the area.

Near where the Red River headed south, a legend said a treasure was buried near a tree and bluff. An old Mexican map showed where the treasure was located. There was also a legend about treasure buried on the Texas side of the river west of Dexter, near Walnut Bend. Another legend has a treasure hidden on the Oklahoma side of Sivell's Bend in Love County.

Starling Treasure

The Starling treasure may be located near Marietta.

Twenty Mule Loads of Gold

See Love County.

MAYES COUNTY

Garden Cache

A Cherokee woman buried her 1852 government payment of $1,000 in $20 gold pieces at her farm. She died without disclosing its location. In 1906, her five grandsons were digging in the garden and uncovered her cache. Her farm was said to have been about fourteen miles east of Pryor in Mayes County or Delaware County.

Grand River Spanish Treasure

Another Spanish treasure was supposed to be located on the Grand River near Pryor.

Henry Starr Treasures

See Le Flore County, "Henry Starr Treasures," as one $100,000 treasure in gold was said to be near Rose or Pryor. The Henry Starr Gang robbed a train at Pryor Creek.

Lacy Mouse's Treasure

See Delaware County.

Lindsay's Treasure

In about 1873, an Indian rancher called Lindsay (Lindsey) lived about sixteen miles southeast of Claremore near Scaley Back (Scaley Rock) Mountain. Lindsay drove his cattle down the Texas Road to Denison, Texas, and sold them for $20,000 or $25,000, with part of it in gold. He was said to have buried the money in a ravine near Chouteau, Mayes County. Lindsay then died the next morning and was found by his uncle from Kansas who had come to see him. The treasure and its hiding site were not found. Another possible burial site was said to be located between Claremore and Lake Claremore. There are several versions of this story.

Lost Gold Mines

See Delaware County.

Meadows Gang Treasure

The Meadows Gang hid treasure of $135,000 in gold and silver (gold bullion) near Pryor. The gang was reportedly captured and hanged. Treasure hunter Andy Moore claimed the treasure was near the old Pryor water tower.

Moore Farm Treasure Found

In Steve Wilson's book *Oklahoma Treasure and Treasure Tales*, treasure hunter Andy Moore related a story about a man coming to his farm in the 1890s looking for treasure. Moore's farm was about fifteen miles northeast of Pryor. Moore allowed him access. The man looked for maybe two weeks in the field and then disappeared. Moore went to his field and found a hole in it with a rock that had rust on it that indicated to him an iron kettle containing treasure had been removed from the hole.

Wooster McCoy's Cache

Cherokee Wooster McCoy was said to have buried $250 in gold and silver coins in the back of his house on a bluff to hide it from outlaws, guerrillas and renegades during the Civil War. McCoy caught pneumonia and died without telling anyone exactly where his money was cached. His sister told this story of her brother's hidden money to another Cherokee, Johnny West. West later told the story to a *Tulsa Daily World* reporter. It appeared in an article called "When There Was Gold in 'Them Thar Hills'" in the March 22, 1931 edition of the *Tulsa Daily World.* The site is likely in Mayes County or Delaware County.

Younger Gang and James Gang Treasure

A Younger Gang and James Gang treasure of more than $20,000 in gold was said to be located near Pryor. Another variation was that the James-Younger Gang treasure of $110,000 in a kettle was rumored to be hidden in a deep hole in Robber's Canyon, about five miles west of Pryor. Jesse James carved a rattlesnake to mark the site of their loot. This is likely another version of the one that follows.

Younger Gang Pryor Loot

Cole Younger's $25,000 of gold coins may have been hidden near Pryor.

MCCURTAIN COUNTY

Treasure Cave

A treasure cave was said to be located at the Little River's Pine Knott Crossing near Valliant or near the Ringold townsite. Inside the cave, weapons, gold watches, jewelry and coins were hidden.

MCINTOSH COUNTY

Honey Springs Treasure

The small community of Honey Springs was the site of the largest battle in Indian Territory during the Civil War. On July 17, 1863, Union General James G. Blunt's army of white, African American and Indian soldiers defeated Confederate Douglas H. Cooper's force of Texas and Indian troops. About two hundred to five hundred soldiers were killed, wounded and captured.

Battle of Honey Springs. *Oklahoma Historical Society*.

In the 1930s, a construction crew was making a new county road through Honey Springs at the site of the Honey Springs Depot, which had been a Confederate camp. This county road was adjacent to the ruins of an old stone building that served as a stage and rest stop on the Texas Road. One of the workers on the construction crew uncovered a treasure dating from the Civil War. The man immediately quit the work crew and left with his find. No one knows what he found. The site is now part of the Honey Springs Battlefield operated by the Oklahoma Historical Society with a museum. When I was young, I participated in an archaeological dig at the site by Gilcrease Museum and also helped catalogue and identify material recovered during that dig and digs by the University of Tulsa/Oklahoma Historical Society.

Opothleyahola's Creek Nation Treasure

As the American Civil War started and Indian Territory became torn apart by the conflict, Upper Creek Chief Opothleyahola reportedly received a payment from the United States government for distribution to tribal members. Chief Opothleyahola was known as Opothleyaholo, Hopoeithleyohola, Hopoth leyahola and Opothle Yahola due to the many English spelling variations of his Creek name. During the War of 1812, at the age of fifteen, Opothleyahola was a Baton Rouge (Red Stick) Creek who fought against the U.S. Army at the Battle of Horseshoe Bend, Alabama.

Opothleyahola was a Creek leader who opposed other Creek Indian leaders who signed treaties exchanging the Creek homeland in the southeastern United States for land in Indian Territory. In the 1830s, Chief Opothleyahola and all the Creek Indians were forced to migrate to Indian Territory in what became known as the Trail of Tears because so many died during the forced migration. Chief Opothleyahola settled near

View from Council Hill. *Author's photo.*

North Fork Town on the Texas Road. He controlled about two thousand acres farmed by his slaves.

D.L. Berryhill later related how when he was eight years old, he watched old Chief Opothleyahola pile $20 gold coins on the kitchen floor of the chief's house. The chief and his close friend placed them in a trunk. One source said it was $159,700 or $160,000 in $20 gold pieces (worth $14 million today if it was about 480 pounds). I suspect $10,000 to $20,000 would be a more likely sum. Chief Opothleyahola ordered four slaves to haul the heavy trunk to a site near Opothleyahola's home in McIntosh County. The slaves excavated a hole and buried the trunk with the gold coins. His home was supposed to have been due west of Checotah at a fork in the road to Rigitsville, south on the Deep Fork River. Another burial site was said to be twelve miles west of Muskogee by a creek with five large four-foot-diameter trees around the burial site. Chief Opothleyahola and his friend murdered the unfortunate slaves to keep the location secret. Opothleyahola was said to have discussed the burial site when he was dying in a Kansas refugee camp.

Joe Grayson, D.L. Berryhill's grandson, related his grandfather's tale to a newspaper reporter decades later. He claimed his grandfather told him where Chief Opothleyahola buried the Creek Nation's treasure. Grayson said it was buried in McIntosh County a few miles southwest of Checotah, just north of the old village of Brush Hill, near a fork in the road. This road fork could be the turnoff to Okmulgee and Mission Hill. Grayson refused to give the exact details of the cache. He wanted the U.S. government to recover the treasure for the Creek tribe. Grayson offered to lead a search party but was unable to get anyone from the U.S. government to join him.

Another version of this story was that the Creek Nation's money was put in a barrel rather than a trunk. There was just one slave who drove Chief Opothleyahola into the hills near his home. Chief Opothleyahola was known to have had a buggy, so maybe they used his buggy rather than a wagon. A hole was dug, and the barrel of gold was hidden in the ground. To conceal the treasure's location, Opothleyahola murdered his slave.

Chief Opothleyahola left his home and led the pro-Union Indians and African Americans to oppose the McIntoshes and their supporters. Daniel N. "Dode" McIntosh and his half brother, Chilly McIntosh, were Confederate Creek leaders. The McIntosh brothers were sons of General William McIntosh, a Lower Creek chief, who had been murdered in Georgia in 1828 by Opothleyahola's followers for signing a treaty that exchanged all Creek lands in Georgia and some Creek lands in Alabama for lands in Indian Territory.

When the Civil War began, Daniel McIntosh raised a Confederate flag over the Creek Agency. The pro-Confederate McIntoshes and other Indian tribes signed treaties with the Confederacy, with Albert Pike being the Confederate Indian agent. Pike was a Confederate brigadier general during the Civil War and a member of the Knights of the Golden Circle (see chapter 4). The Confederate Creeks formed the Confederate First Creek Regiment under Colonel Daniel McIntosh and Lieutenant Colonel Chilly McIntosh.

After the Civil War broke out, the Creek Nation, Choctaw Nation, Seminole Nation, Cherokee Nation and a number of Indian tribes allied themselves with the Confederacy. Being originally from the South but transplanted to Indian Territory during Indian removal, many Native

Chief Opothleyahola. *Library of Congress*.

Americans had more ties and sympathy for the Confederate States of America. Pro-Union Indians from the Seminole, Chickasaw, Choctaw and other Indian tribes, as well as free African Americans, joined Chief Opothleyahola and the Union Creeks. Opothleyahola's pro-Union group contained about 1,500 Indian warriors, 700 African American freemen and slaves and many women, old people and children. The newly formed Confederate government and military forces feared an attack from Opothleyahola's pro-Union Indians and African Americans. White Confederate troops from Texas and Arkansas came into the Indian nations to support the Confederate Creek, Chickasaw, Choctaw, Cherokee, Seminole and other newly formed Confederate Indian units there.

Chief Opothleyahola, who was about sixty-two, knew the pro-Union Indians were likely to be attacked soon. He ordered the pro-Union Indians to hide their valuables and march with him for the safety of Union Kansas. Confederate Texas, Arkansas and Indian forces attacked Opothleyahola's band in three battles in the winter of 1861.

The Battle of Twin Mounds or Round Mountain took place on November 20, 1861 (see Payne County, "Twin Mounds Treasures"). Chief Opothleyahola was forced to abandon his buggy along with many of his followers' wagons after successfully defeating the Confederates. On December 9, 1861, in present Tulsa County, the Battle of Caving Banks or Chusto-Talash took place along Bird Creek. Several hundred pro-Union warriors were killed and wounded. Several hundred Cherokees in Drew's Regiment of Cherokee Mounted Rifles changed sides and joined Opothleyahola's band of Union Indians. Opothleyahola's band retreated closer to Kansas. At the next battle on December 26, 1861, Opothleyahola's band was completely defeated. At the Battle of Chustenahlah or Patriot's Hills in present Osage County, the Union Indians lost 250 warriors killed and 160 women and children captured, along with most of their livestock and worldly goods. Opothleyahola's Creek Indian friend, who was also said to have helped bury the Creek Nation gold, was killed in one of these fights.

Chief Opothleyahola and his defeated followers scattered in disorganized desperate groups toward Kansas with Confederate forces attacking many of these groups amid bitterly cold weather. The survivors stumbled into Kansas. At Roe's Fort, just south of Belmont, Kansas, the Indian refugees gathered in a crude refugee camp. As they waited for aid from the U.S. government, hundreds of Indian and African American refugees grew sick and died during the long cold winter. In their first two months in Kansas, Chief Opothleyahola's daughter died, along with 240 Creek followers.

Chief Opothleyahola died in the winter of 1863. Chief Opothleyahola and his daughter were both buried in Belmont, Kansas. For more than a century, treasure hunters have extensively searched the area of Chief Opothleyahola's plantation and other areas. No one has ever reported finding the Creek Nation treasure.

Standing Rock Treasure

There was a legend that Spaniards buried $200,000 worth of gold in a cave near Standing Rock during an Indian attack. Standing Rock was a marker on the California Road near the Texas Road that connected Kansas to Texas through the Indian nations.

Standing Rock is a large piece of sandstone broken off from an outcrop that ended up in the Canadian River. It had a base of about one hundred feet and once towered forty feet above the Canadian River. Some Indians were said to have found hidden gold there, which they took to Fort Smith and sold. Standing Rock is located two miles below the junction of the North Canadian River and South Canadian River and is now under Lake Eufaula, which was constructed from 1956 to 1964. Standing Rock had a turtle and a triangle with a handle carved on it.

Over the centuries, many people searched for treasure near Standing Rock. Early U.S. military soldiers Major William Bradford and Colonel Mathew Arbuckle scouted the area with their troops looking for Spanish treasure. Before World War II, a large treasure hunting expedition from Texas spent about a year looking for treasure in the area, including making deals with the area's landowners.

There was another version of this story, which had the treasure buried south of Standing Rock on the north bank of Piney Creek. It was supposed to have been buried near a bluff and under a large birch tree. In 1964, the *Tulsa Daily World* wrote that Wilbert Martin of Tulsa found a small chunk of silver at the base of an old oak tree with a carved arrowhead on the tree pointing down in the area before Standing Rock was inundated by Lake Eufaula. Symbols on nearby trees included an arrowhead and a turtle. A boulder nearby had a triangle carved into it.

Walter Grayson Treasure

See Okfuskee County.

MURRAY COUNTY

Eight Mile Creek Treasure

See Garvin County.

Fort Arbuckle Treasure

See Garvin County.

Pack Train Treasure

A pack train worth $50 million may have been attacked in the Arbuckle Mountains, Murray County, and the treasure of gold and silver bars and coins and plate were hidden.

Spanish Silver

Thirteen mule loads of silver was supposedly cached in a cave some seven miles west and five miles south of Davis.

MUSKOGEE COUNTY

Dr. John J. Hayes's Lost Gold

See Haskell County.

Holt Treasure

See Sequoyah County.

NOBLE COUNTY

Red Rock Post Office Loot

In 1901, the B.F. Swarts Store and post office in the small community of Red Rock, Oklahoma Territory, was robbed by Ben Craven and Bert Welty of about $1,200 in gold and silver coins. If it was all coins, it would have weighed one hundred pounds or more. The postmaster was killed during the robbery. The two robbers escaped in a wagon that later tipped over in a gully. Welty was shot by his partner, Craven, and left for dead. Welty, however, was not dead. He made it to a nearby farm, where he got medical help. Craven rode east with two horses and the loot. He was arrested and went to prison for life for the robbery at Red Rock and other criminal actions. The loot disappeared, according to this version of the tale.

Buss Smith's article "Buried Loot at Red Rock" in *True Treasure* magazine detailed his family's story about the robbery committed by Bert Welty and Ben Craven. It was different in key parts than the above story. Welty showed up seventeen years after the robbery at Red Rock at the home of his second cousin Fred Smith, who lived about three miles west of Altona, Kingfisher County. Welty's version of what happened was that he had fallen down with the $1,200 in loot and had been accidentally shot by Craven, who thought he was someone else chasing him. Welty was dazed, as he had buckshot in his face and elsewhere. Welty fled with the loot for about two miles east of Red Rock. He found a cowboy camp with an iron pot with a lid in the camp. Welty took the iron pot, put the loot in it and buried it under a cottonwood tree.

Fred Smith and Bert Welty spent several weeks in 1918 looking unsuccessfully for the $1,200 cache. The land had changed a lot, and Bert Welty's memory was poor. The treasure was supposed to be east of a hill or draw about one and a half miles east of Red Rock. There were also other draws to the northeast and southeast of Red Rock, so it was possible that they did not look in the right place. Fred Smith told his son about the lost loot and wanted to look for it later, but he never did. His son Buss Smith, who wrote the article, left Oklahoma in 1940 and returned in 1965 but could not find the treasure.

Red Rock Train Loot

On June 1, 1892, the Doolin-Dalton Gang robbed a Santa Fe Railroad train at Red Rock. Red Rock is on the Otoe Indian Reservation and located between I-35 and U.S. 177, just north of I-44 (Turner Turnpike). Rumors that a train was going to be robbed there caused the first southbound train to have a band of armed lawmen aboard. The Doolin-Dalton Gang let the first train pass, but a second train that arrived shortly thereafter was stopped and robbed. A fifteen-minute gunfight took place with two armed guards on the train before they surrendered. It was at first claimed that $50,000 was stolen. Emmett Dalton reported that $11,000 was taken. The railroad reported only $1,600 stolen in its records—but this could have just been the railroad's loss and not any other parties' money. There was also a report of $19,000 in loot being taken at the robbery. The robbers' loot was said to have been buried east of Red Rock, although it may have just been the heavy coins. The robbers would have wanted to lighten the load on their horses since a posse would be after them.

NOWATA COUNTY

Dalton Gang $9,000 Cache

The Dalton Gang was said to have had $9,000 when they left Tulsa heading to rob the banks in Coffeyville, Kansas, according to Emmett Dalton. Bailey C. Hanes's book *Bill Doolin Outlaw I.T.* states that a gang inventory showed $920 in assets, but it is unclear when this inventory was done. Normally, the loot would have been split among the gang members and they would hide their loot separately. Outlaw Bill Doolin decided not to join the Dalton Gang for this twin banks robbery. There were several areas between Tulsa and Coffeyville, Kansas, where the Dalton Gang may have stopped and buried its funds.

Somewhere on Onion Creek, just below South Coffeyville, is where the Dalton Gang camped before going in to rob the Coffeyville banks. They spent the previous night on upper Hickory Creek, some twelve miles from Coffeyville. Other possible locations are near Coodey's Bluff and Lightning Creek near the Verdigris River, which is southeast of Nowata, Nowata County. This would be in or near Oologah Lake, which was built by the U.S. Army Corps of Engineers between 1951 and 1974. Other locations could be in Tulsa County near Sand Springs. The Dalton Gang that rode to rob Coffeyville consisted of Bob Dalton, Emmett Dalton, Grat Dalton, Dick Broadwell and Bill Powers.

On the morning of October 6, 1892, the five outlaws rode from their camp on Onion Creek and robbed the First National Bank and C.M. Condon &

Dalton Gang members killed at Coffeyville. *Oklahoma Historical Society.*

Company's Bank. At first they were successful and got more than $20,000, but the citizens recognized a robbery was being committed. For the next fifteen minutes, a gun battle ensued. When it was over, only Emmett Dalton survived from the gang, but he had twenty-three wounds in his body and was thought to be dying. Three Coffeyville citizens were killed, and three others were wounded. The $20,000 was recovered, along with some extra cash found in the robbers' pockets.

Although Emmett Dalton was said to have claimed that they had hidden $9,000 before entering Coffeyville, he said this while badly wounded and on death's door. Some claimed the gang had no money. The gang had committed a number of train and other robberies that year. Whatever money they had, it would have made a lot of sense to cache most of it. They expected to be chased by a posse after they robbed the Coffeyville banks. Instead of the gang hiding money in one place, it is likely the individual outlaws hid their loot in separate stashes.

Miners' Lost Gold

Near South Coffeyville, a wagon containing more than $50,000 in gold coins and nuggets was said to have overturned at a crossing of the Verdigris River. The water scattered the gold, and the Montana miners were only able to recover a small amount of the gold. The location is likely to have been east of present South Coffeyville, although some published material puts it one mile south of South Coffeyville, which is not on the Verdigris River.

OKFUSKEE COUNTY

California Miners' Gold

Miners returning from California with gold were supposed to have buried their gold near Dog Ford on the North Canadian River. This might be the same area as Trader Thomas James's Cache.

The Devil's Half Acre

About $278,000 in Spanish gold (gold concentrate) was reportedly hidden in a mine in kegs near where two creeks joined, about eight miles south of an oxbow lake. This area was said to be on the North Canadian River near Okemah. An Indian attack killed all the Spaniards but one, who made it safely back to Mexico. The survivor died, and the location was lost. Many years later, six men were looking for the mine in the area. In another version of this story, the lost gold mine was about eight miles south of Okemah. There are no gold-bearing formations in this area, so the gold mine is impossible.

Trader Thomas James's Cache

One of the first successful trading expeditions from the United States to Santa Fe, Mexico (now New Mexico), was the Glenn and Fowler Expedition. Mexico became an independent nation after years of revolution against Spain and finally allowed trade with the United States along land routes. The Glenn and Fowler Expedition successfully returned to St. Louis from Santa Fe in the summer of 1822. The traders then split up over disagreements. Thomas James was a trapper, merchant, trader and explorer with this expedition.

Thomas James gathered twenty-two men for his expedition to trade with the Comanches in present western Oklahoma. He purchased $5,500 worth of trade goods on credit in St. Louis, Missouri, to exchange for Comanche furs. In the fall of 1822, the James Expedition left St. Louis and went down the Mississippi River. The expedition journeyed up the Arkansas River and then up the Canadian River with its trade goods in a keelboat. Part of the trading expedition rode horses along the Canadian River with difficulty in the rough wooded country as the keelboat slowly went upstream.

For five days, the James Expedition traveled up the Canadian River and North Canadian River (North Fork of the Canadian River). The keelboat had trouble navigating the many sandbars and snags in the very winding river. In many places, the river was shallow with numerous rapids. Finally, the North Canadian River proved too difficult to make any progress. James wrote that the keelboat could sometimes only make one hundred yards a day. A rapids or falls finally blocked the keelboat. In his book *Three Years Among the Indians and Mexicans*, Thomas James wrote that "the boat was at length stopped entirely by a rapid which we could not ascend. We made first the boat to trees with strong ropes, put our bear and deer skins into it, and buried the heaviest hardware in the ground, where it probably remains to this day as I never returned to its place of concealment."

Thomas James and his men built three small boats or pirogues to carry their remaining goods upriver. Some goods were put on five packhorses. Having more trading goods than they could now transport, James and his men cached their heaviest trade goods for later retrieval. Many of the horses he obtained in trading died of disease and thus brought him no profit.

James returned to southern Illinois and settled down. The unsuccessful trading expedition bankrupted him, as he ended up owing creditors more than $12,000. He never returned to trading. He became an Illinois militia general in 1825, served in the Illinois legislature and later became the postmaster of Monroe County, Illinois. He was a major in the Black Hawk War in 1832. He profited from iron mining and smelting. James's book *Three Years Among the Indians and Mexicans* was published in 1846. He died in 1847.

Some historians believe the rapids where Thomas James cached his trade goods was at Old Dog Ford on the North Canadian River in Seminole County and Okfuskee County. Old Dog Ford was on the old trail that ran north to south through old Arbeka town.

Walter Grayson Treasure

Wealthy Creek Walter "Watt" Grayson was captured by three white outlaws at his home. A rope was put around his head, and he was hanged seven times to the point of passing out, as the outlaws were determined Grayson would disclose where he hid his money. The outlaws then hanged his wife three times. To save her life, Walter Grayson told where his fortune was buried. He was robbed of $30,000 in gold coins on the night of November 19, 1873. Grayson lived near Eufaula, north of the Canadian River. Several locations have been given as the site of Walter Grayson's home, including near Grayson. There is speculation the robbers may have been from Texas or part of Belle Starr's gang, which lived at nearby Younger's Bend. Outlaw Dan Evans was arrested and hanged at Fort Smith on September 3, 1875, for murdering a cowboy. Evans claimed that he, Sam Wilder and James W. Reed had robbed Walter Grayson. Reed was one of Quantrill's Confederate guerrillas during the Civil War, a member of the Younger Gang and Belle Starr's husband. Some believe the outlaws may have hidden their loot on the Canadian River near Eufaula, McIntosh County.

OKLAHOMA COUNTY

Lost Creek Treasure

In Oklahoma City, about five miles from downtown on the east branch of Lost Creek near Western Avenue, forty jack loads of gold bullion were said to have been buried by a party of Mexicans during an Indian attack at a spring or arroyo. The party was from Santa Fe, New Mexico, heading to St. Louis, Missouri. Settlers in 1895–96 were reported to have searched for the gold bullion. The settlers dug a hole on the east branch of Lost Creek at a spring, but the influx of water prevented them from digging deeper. Spanish relics and old human bones have been uncovered in this area, giving some credence to this story.

OSAGE COUNTY

Frank Goldie's Gold

Frank Goldie lived on a farm with his wife near Springfield, Missouri. In about 1850, Frank Goldie left for the California gold fields. He worked mining claims on the Mokelumne River, in the San Joaquin Valley and Coon Hollow areas. Goldie was very successful. Early in 1862, he sold his California mining claims and supposedly loaded four hundred pounds in gold dust worth about $100,000 in canvas bags in a wagon. At the time of this writing, Frank Goldie's treasure could be worth about $8 million. He had a second wagon to carry supplies that was driven by an unsuccessful prospector wanting to return to Pennsylvania. Goldie joined a wagon train heading east; he may have been elected captain of the wagon train.

From near present Wichita, Kansas, a band of Pawnee Indians trailed the wagon train. One of the Pawnees had seen or heard about Goldie's gold. Pawnee Indians were generally pro-Union during the Civil War. The Pawnees attacked the wagon train on the trail in the Osage Hills near the present location of Pawhuska. The wagon train was quickly overrun and its people massacred. Goldie fled with livestock and maybe his wagon. The Pawnees found Goldie's tracks leading away from the wagon train and followed him. Near the Caney River, Goldie hid his gold in a forest. He was said to have buried his gold between a hill that is now called Artillery Mound to the north and a large tree trunk to the south with two trees growing out of it. Goldie inserted his musket in the hollow tree to mark the location. He turned his livestock free and chased them off in the opposite direction he planned to travel. The Pawnees followed the released livestock, and Goldie escaped.

After making his way to his Missouri home, Goldie grew very sick and drew a crude map for his wife showing the gold's location before he died. The Civil War was depopulating much of Missouri at this time. Homes were burned, and people became refugees. Guerrilla gangs roamed the countryside. Frank Goldie's wife trusted no one with the news of the buried gold. Her son was too young to hunt for his father's gold. All along the border of Kansas, Missouri and the Indian nations, Union and Confederate soldiers were in active conflict. Guerrillas, outlaws and desperate people were everywhere.

In 1882, Goldie's son arrived at the farm of an Osage named Joe Boulanger. Young Goldie hunted for the markers on his father's map to find the gold. He found the marker of Artillery Mound, but the other markers were not found. There had been a forest there in 1862, but twenty years later, the trees were gone. Goldie's son was told by Boulanger that he had cut down the trees in order to farm the land. Boulanger recalled the key large tree trunk with two trees growing out of it, as well as the old musket he found in the hollow tree. For permission to search on Boulanger's land, Goldie's son agreed to share the gold with Boulanger. Goldie's son worked long days digging and probing Boulanger's farm without any success.

His son finally gave up searching. He gave Boulanger a copy of the map. Boulanger promised that if the gold was discovered, part of it would belong to young Goldie's mother. Boulanger never looked for the gold, but it was evident that Goldie's son told others about the lost gold. In 1901, a hole was found in Boulanger's cornfield. Over several nights, someone deepened the hole. Soon, other holes showed up on his land, as someone was desperately searching for the gold. Boulanger reported the trespassing to the Osage Indian agent, and several Osage policemen were posted to guard his land. No more holes occurred, so whoever was digging left. I suspect Goldie may have been a nickname in this story and Goldie had another last name.

Martin Brothers' Gold

Outlaw brothers Sam and Will Martin performed a number of robberies in northwestern Oklahoma Territory in present Woods County, Kingfisher County and other areas. On March 2, 1903, the Martin brothers robbed the Rock Island Depot in Hennessey and killed Gusy Gravett. Gravett was at the depot to pick up his niece from the train. Several posses chased the two outlaws all over Oklahoma Territory for several months. Near Liza Creek about three miles west and south of Bartlesville, the Martin brothers even robbed a large number of people (maybe seventy-five to one hundred) heading to church one Sunday. It was said they got less than $5,000 in addition to a gold watch and three saddled horses. Seeing that Oklahoma Territory was too hot for them to stay in, the outlaws crossed the Arkansas River into the Osage Indian Reservation, which later became Osage County. They rode two stolen horses and had a third horse to carry supplies and their loot.

About three miles southwest of Pawhuska, a party of Osages on Bird Creek saw one of the outlaws come to Bird Creek to get some water for his camp on August 3, 1903. He kept to himself and went over a rise with a heavy burlap sack. He returned sometime later, and the burlap sack appeared empty. The man then rode off. The Osages let the lawmen in Pawhuska know about the white stranger since outlaws had been terrorizing the area.

Deputy U.S. Marshal Wiley Haines, Osage Police Chief Warren Bennett and Osage policeman Henry Majors gathered a posse and went to the Bird Creek area to investigate. The posse began looking for where the burlap sack might have been emptied. They found outlaws Sam Martin, Will Martin and Clarence Simmons on a knoll called Wooster's Mound several miles southeast of Pawhuska. The outlaws were lying on the ground with their heads on their saddles. Their horses were tied to the nearby tree. The outlaws and the lawmen fired at one another. Will Martin was shot in the jaw and died immediately, while Sam Martin was severely wounded in the shoulder. Clarence Simmons escaped. Deputy U.S. Marshal Wiley G. Haines was wounded in the gunfight. The lawmen recovered some stolen loot, two rifles, four pistols, a lot of ammunition and three horses. They did not find a great amount of money.

Sam Martin was taken back to Pawhuska, where he soon died after indicating they had hidden their loot near Bird Creek. A few coins have been found in the area, which makes some believe the bulk of the money is still hidden. The loot was said to have been $14,000 in gold and silver coins. This amount of gold and silver coins would have been very heavy—too heavy to be carried easily in a burlap bag. Some of their loot would have been in currency in 1903. It is also likely that they could have buried it somewhere else or split it up among the robbers.

Outlaw Bullion

An outlaw gang was supposed to have buried gold bullion on Bird Creek near Pearsonia.

Outlaw Loot

The *Blackwell Morning Tribute* of September 15, 1932, reported an outlaw treasure was buried on the H. Kohlmeyar Farm near Barnsdall after the landowner discovered several men digging at night on his farm. Although these men were armed, they were arrested. The diggers said they were hunting for $80,000 in outlaw treasure. There was no indication they found it.

Robbers' Caches

Several robber caches may have been hidden near Nelagoney.

Spanish Silver Bullion

Spanish (or Mexican) silver bullion was supposedly cached near Lost Creek in the Osage Hills in the early 1800s. The Spaniards were en route to New Orleans with their treasure when they were attacked by Osages near Woolaroc, the site of the Frank Phillips Ranch, which now contains museums and a wildlife refuge.

OTTAWA COUNTY

Gambler's Cache

A gambler reportedly cached some gold coins near the Spring River, probably in Ottawa County. He was killed in a saloon fight shortly thereafter.

Mexican Miner Treasure

See Delaware County.

Mexican Treasure at Locust Grove

Peoria Chief Baptiste Peoria told a story that the locust grove located east of the I-44 interchange near Miami was the site of where a Mexican party with three burros carrying gold and silver were being chased by Indians. The Mexican party buried their treasure and planted locust trees to mark the location. Locust trees were not native to this area. Chief Peoria and some of his tribe settled in what was called Peoria about six to seven miles east of Miami. This is likely not a true story but one created by a gifted storyteller.

Shoemaker's Treasure

A German shoemaker's treasure may be hidden at Devil's Promenade, which is a large rocky area where Rock Creek empties into the Spring River. The shoemaker was frugal and cached his gold and silver coins in a box. He hid the treasure box in a crevice or small cave at or near the Devil's Promenade, about six miles east of Quapaw. He was said to have told his friend, a Piankeshaw (considered by some to be part of the Miami or Peoria tribe) Indian who lived near Miami, Oklahoma, about what he had done. The Piankeshaws had settled in that area as part of the Indian removal system. The shoemaker suddenly got ill and died. The Indian passed down the story over the years.

Spanish Diggings

The Spanish were said to have mined valuable minerals in Ottawa County. This was probably lead and zinc, as Ottawa County is in the Ozark Lead and Zinc Belt. Native Americans were also known to have dug for flint to make arrowheads and other implements. Mine shafts that were called Spanish diggings are actually Indian flint mines.

PAWNEE COUNTY

Outlaw Hideouts

See Payne County.

Twin Mounds Treasures

See Payne County.

PAYNE COUNTY

Doolin-Dalton Gang's Ingalls Area

The Doolin-Dalton Gang committed a number of robberies with much loot, including $11,000 from a Spearsville, Kansas bank; $14,000 from a Cimarron, Kansas bank; $15,000 from Southwest City, Missouri; and a few thousand dollars from a bank in Pawnee, Indian Territory. In 1893, the newly established small town of Ingalls, Oklahoma Territory, had a post office, the OK Hotel, bars (Ransom & Murray Saloon), a livery stable and other places of outlaw amusement. The Dunn brothers' Rockfort was about eighteen miles east of Ingalls. The gang was often in Ingalls when not robbing trains and other people. Doolin-Dalton Gang hideouts were located nearby. Their hideouts were the Deer Creek overhang near the Cimarron River, Dunn Ranch, Bar X Ranch and Cowboy Flat. Marshal Red Lucas came to Ingalls, and unknowingly, the outlaws played poker with him. Marshal Lucas was looking for the outlaws and lost no time in raising a posse of lawmen to clean out the outlaw nest.

On the morning of August 31, 1893, the Doolin-Dalton Gang consisted of Bill Dalton, Bill Doolin, Roy "Arkansas Tom Jones" Daugherty, Bob Yocum, Dan "Dynamite Dick" Clifton, George "Bitter Creek"/"Slaughter's Kid" Newcomb, William "Tulsa Jack" Blake, George "Red Buck" Weightman and a few others in Ingalls. Most had been cowboys at the nearby Halsell Ranch. Newcomb had been a cowboy on C.J. Slaughter's Long S. Ranch in Colorado and got one of his nicknames from there.

The lawmen came into town in three covered wagons, as there were a lot of wagons in the area for an upcoming land run. They hoped to escape notice until they were ready to capture the outlaws. Deputy U.S. Marshals Dick Speed, Hamilton "Ham" Huestron, Henry Keller, George Cox, M.A. Iason and Hi Thompson were in one group from Stillwater. Another group from Guthrie consisted of Deputy U.S. Marshals Jim Masterson (brother of the famous Doc Masterson of OK Corral fame), Isaac A. Steel, J.S. Burke, Lafe Shadley and John Hixon. A third group of marshals arrived after the gunfight.

U.S. Marshals Dick Speed, Thomas J. (Tom or T.J.) Huestron (brother of Hamilton "Ham" Huestron) and Lafe Shadley were killed in the gunfight. Arkansas Tom was trapped in the OK Hotel and eventually surrendered. Two barkeepers were wounded and a town citizen killed. Bitter Creek was wounded when a bullet from Deputy Dick Speed hit Bitter Creek's rifle and a fragment hit Bitter Creek in the leg. As Bitter Creek escaped on his horse, a bullet fired by Tom Huestron hit Bitter Creek. Bitter Creek and the other outlaws escaped on their horses. Since the lawmen had come in wagons, they were not able to quickly chase the outlaws. The surviving lawmen began searching for the outlaws. The full force of the law eventually tracked them down.

Bill Dalton was killed in June 1894. Bill Doolin had a wife, Edith, and a young son. Doolin was staying with his wife's father, J.W. Ellsworth, who was the Lawson postmaster. Doolin was killed at the Eagle Creek bridge near Lawson on August 23, 1895, by lawman Heck Thomas and a posse, which included the Dunn brothers. William "Tulsa Jack" Blake was killed in a gunfight on April 4, 1895. George "Red Buck" Weightman was killed on March 4, 1896, by lawmen. Dynamite Dick Clifton was killed in 1897 by lawmen. Arkansas Tom Jones Daugherty was killed in 1924 while resisting arrest. These outlaws likely hid loot before being killed.

Outlaw Hideouts

The Bar X Bar Ranch had the Borden blockhouse in case of attack. The Jordan Triangle was an area of 105,0000 acres of leased land between the Arkansas River and Cimarron River, with the Pawnee Reservation on the west. The ranch house was on Turkey Creek near Pawnee. It was used by the Doolin-Dalton Gang as a hideout. The Dunn Ranch was a hideout used by members of the Doolin-Dalton Gang. It was on Council Creek about two and a half miles southeast of Ingalls. Some of the Dunn brothers rode with outlaws. On May 1, 1895, Charley Pierce and Bitter Creek Newcomb rode to the Dunn Ranch, ate dinner and then went to sleep upstairs. Since a $5,000 bounty was offered for these two outlaws, the Dunn brothers decided to kill them for the reward. In the early morning of May 2, 1895, Bee Dunn and John Dunn went silently upstairs with a shotgun and a Winchester rifle and opened fire on the two sleeping outlaws.

The bodies of the two outlaws were placed on a wagon and taken to Guthrie, where the Dunns claimed the reward money. On the way, it appears one of them recovered and asked for help but was shot again by the Dunns. In Pierce's pockets were two knives, some coins, a rabbit's foot and twenty-six Winchester shells. Bitter Creek was said to have had an empty Wells Fargo money bag in his saddlebag. If they had much money, it was likely the Dunns took it. It is just as likely that both outlaws hid some of their money nearby. It is hard to believe the outlaws had traveled with so little money.

Twin Mounds Treasures

During the flight of Chief Opothleyahola's Union Indians toward Kansas during the Civil War, Creek Chief Paseola was said to also have a sum of $60,000 with him before the first battle with Confederate forces at Round Mountain or Twin Mounds on November 20, 1861. When Confederate soldiers attacked, Chief Paseola ordered two Union Indians to load his money on a horse and bury the treasure near Twin Mounds. Twin Mounds is a distinctive pair of hills eighteen miles east of Stillwater. The two Indians who buried the treasure died during Opothleyahola's retreat to Kansas. This story is likely a variation of Opothleyahola's Creek Nation Treasure in McIntosh County. My guess is that Chief Paseola is actually Chief Yahola and whoever wrote the story down used the wrong spelling. It could also be another Indian leader who hid his or his group's money, but I have not found this name in my research. Goab Childers, who was a fourteen-year-old boy at the time of the Battle of Twin Mounds, told James Fleming this story in 1887.

Twin Mounds. *Oklahoma Historical Society.*

A paymaster's treasure of $11,000 in gold coins was said to have been hidden near Twin Mounds near Jennings, in Pawnee County or Payne County. Indians attacked the soldiers between the hills, and five soldiers escaped.

Another battle in 1869 between Texas Rangers and cattle and horse thieves from Texas was also said to have occurred at Twin Mounds. There is a lot of confusion over battles and when they took place at this site.

PONTOTOC COUNTY

Marshall Treasure

Ben Marshall, a wealthy Indian also called Captain Kidd, was said to have hidden a treasure of about $50,000 or $60,000 in gold in Pontotoc County near Stonewall. He had sold his land in Alabama, which later became Girard, Alabama. He was supposed to have owned many slaves. After Indian removal, he settled in an area called the Point between the Verdigris River and Arkansas River in Wagoner County. During the Civil War, Marshall became a refugee at Stonewall, where he was said to have secretly buried his treasure and then died.

Spanish Treasures

About $30 million worth of Spanish mission treasure may be hidden north of the Red River in Pontotoc County. Also, near Ada, $1 million in Spanish gold was rumored to have been cached on the Spanish Trail.

PUSHMATAHA COUNTY

Glass Jars Treasure

The glass jars treasure was supposed to be located near Sulphur Canyon Bridge near Clayton.

Jackfork Mountains Mines

Indian mines were said to be located in the Jackfork Mountains of western Pushmataha County. There is a story that during construction of the Indian Nations Turnpike near Jumbo, the road cut through mineralized granite.

Jewelry Store Loot

Loot from a jewelry store robbery was rumored to be in the western Kiamichi Mountains.

Lost Kiamichi Mountains Mines

There is a story that in 1783, French trader Gai Genard heard about a Caddo Indian mine along the Kiamichi River near Clayton. The French called the Kiamichi River La Riviere La Mine or Mine River. The Lost French Silver Mine and the Lost Caddo Mine were supposed to be in this area.

In the Kiamichi Mountains, twelve Choctaws gathered outside circuit riding Reverend W.J.B. Lloyd's cabin one morning in 1865 during a camp meeting. Choctaw Simeon Crusher gave the preacher the peace sign and said, "We want nothing. We are here to give." The Choctaws swore Preacher Lloyd to secrecy. The Choctaws offered to provide for the preacher's simple needs if he would follow them deep into the hills. At the mouth of a small gorge or canyon, several large rocks were moved, revealing an outcropping with veins of gold that filled a fissure in the rock.

The Choctaws and the preacher took only enough gold to meet their minimum needs. Finally, the gold was exhausted without blasting the rock away to go deeper. The mine was sealed with rocks and gravel, and they never did further work on the mine. Reverend Lloyd was the next to the last of the thirteen men associated with the mine to die.

Many years later, when the Choctaws started digging another mine, Choctaw Chief Allen Wright was said to have ordered them to cease mining, and the shaft was filled with stones and hidden. The second mine was supposed to have an owl carved into an overlooking rock and is known as the Lost Sky Pilot Mine. The last mining from the site was said to have taken place about 1884. No appreciable amount of gold has yet to be authenticated as being mined in eastern Oklahoma. Eastern Oklahoma's surface or near-surface rocks are sedimentary with complex faulting in places, which could have mineral deposits.

Missing Safe

In the 1880s to 1890, a St. Louis–San Francisco Railroad (Katy) train was reportedly robbed near the small community of Kosoma (Kasumi) north of Antlers on Buck Creek. A safe on board the train containing $3,000 in gold coins was taken in the robbery along with the mail sacks. The robbers were captured and sent to prison. Buckles said to be part of the mail sacks were found nearby. In 1920, two boys supposedly found a safe under a pile of rocks north of Kosoma within three miles of where Buck Creek and Kiamishi River join. The boys could not open it and covered the safe with rocks. They never could find it again. If there was in fact $3,000 in gold coins (worth about $20.50 per ounce in just gold value in 1890), today with the price of gold at about $1,700 per ounce that treasure would be worth about $248,000!

Seven Devils Mountains Treasures

An outlaw who was later hanged in Hugo was said to have hidden $50,000 in gold coins near a cliff in the Seven Devils Mountains (Kiamichi Mountains) near Rattan. The gold came from a stagecoach robbery in the 1890s. The story was that he took the gold coins out of the strongbox and then hid them. The outlaw was captured and tried to cut a deal with a deputy sheriff. The outlaw gave directions to the cache on the condition that if the deputy sheriff found the loot, he would set the outlaw free. When the deputy sheriff returned from his search, the outlaw was hanged. The deputy remained in town and never seemed to have had a lot of money. Michael Paul Henson quoted complex directions to the site in an article called "Lost Treasure in Oklahoma," which was published in *Lost Treasure* magazine.

Another more likely treasure story has $80,000 ($75,000) in gold coins in a copper box hidden in a cave on a cliff or rocky ledge half a mile east of a cabin about eighteen miles northeast of Rattan near Cloudy. The treasure was owned by Captain T.M., whose last name has not come down in print. He may have been an Indian. Captain T.M. was married to an Indian woman who did not speak English. Captain T.M., who died in 1902, hid the box with the coins in a place unknown to his wife. According to his wife, he would travel east from the cabin and then return from the north, and the travel time took about a half hour. Sometimes he would go north and then return from the east. Paris, Texas treasure hunters Charles Golden and Jack Kimball unsuccessfully looked for this treasure for several years along with B.A. Huddleston. Huddleston wrote an article, "$80,000 Hoard in the Oklahoma Hills," for *True Treasure* on their search. They looked in the Little River, Devil's Backbone Mountain, Bear Canyon and Rattlesnake Canyon areas without finding the treasure.

ROGER MILLS COUNTY

Lost Gold

In the Antelope Hills, Spanish gold may have been hidden near Red Cloud. This was based on local newspaper stories in the *Guyman Herald*, which reported that a large gold nugget was recovered in 1909 near Butler.

Another version of this story was that Mexican miners from Colorado gold mines were traveling through the Antelope Hills in the 1850s when they were attacked by Comanches and Cheyennes northwest of present Crawford. The gold was hidden in a cave. Only two of the Mexican miners escaped. In 1905, a Mexican who claimed to be the son-in-law of one of the survivors arrived in the area with a map. He spent several months looking for the gold without success.

ROGERS COUNTY

Corncrib Treasure

In the 1870s, $800 was said to have been taken in a robbery in Salina. The loot was supposedly buried in an Indian corncrib in the now-vanished Cherokee village of Sand Town on the east side of the Verdigris River near its junction with Bird Creek. Sand Town was north of old U.S. 66 between Catoosa and Verdigris.

Lindsay's Treasure

See Mayes County.

$37,500 Found Treasure

In January 1913, George Hardstock was digging a ditch for a pipeline near Oglesby, not far from Claremore, when he hit a metal object at about two feet of depth. To his amazement, as he cleared off the dirt from the object, he discovered more than one hundred pounds of coins in several rotted bags. He recovered $37,300 in $20 gold coins and $200 in silver coins. Kit Dalton, who was related to members of the Dalton Gang and also claimed to be a member of the James Gang, later asserted the found treasure was part of a $70,000 holdup. The treasure found was buried near a tree, but the gang was unable to locate the markers to recover it.

SEMINOLE COUNTY

Found Silver Ingots

Near Seminole, Dayne Chastain found thirty-five silver ingots with "1714" on them after finding some carvings in the area. Each eight-ounce ingot was 3 inches long, 1.25 inches wide and 0.5 inch deep.

Possible Treasure Markers

Ten miles northeast of Seminole, rocks contain carvings of snakes, horses and a boot spur that some believe mark buried treasure nearby.

Trader Thomas James's Cache

See Okfuskee County.

SEQUOYAH COUNTY

Brushy Mountain Treasure

About $12 million in Spanish treasure was supposedly buried on Brushy Mountain, just north of Sallisaw. Another version of this story was that the treasure was that of a Mexican bandit. An old sheepskin map was reportedly brought by Spaniards from Mexico to Brushy Mountain to look for the markers that indicated where the treasure was hidden.

Holt Treasure

The pro-Confederate Cherokee Holt family had a plantation on the Arkansas River across from Webbers Falls. Captain Charles H. Holt was the commander of the First Cherokee Squadron of Mounted Volunteers (Holt's Squadron) during the Civil War. On December 12, 1862, Holt's Squadron was enlisted into the Confederate army. The Holt family silverware and cash were buried on the Holt Place before the family fled from the Cherokee Nation due to Union occupation. The treasure was not said to have been found after the Civil War. It could be in Sequoyah County or Muskogee County.

Lee's Creek Treasure

A treasure was reportedly buried on Lee's Creek just west of the Oklahoma-Arkansas state line. Frenchmen were said to have hidden their treasure in a cave three miles north of Lee's Creek Crossing when Arapahos attacked them. A variation of this story was that the Arapaho Indians killed all the Frenchmen and the Arapahos hid the treasure in the cave.

Another story version claimed Spaniards with seven burro loads of gold were attacked about four miles north of Nicut at Lee's Crossing a mile west or downstream at Lee's Creek Slough. The twelve Spaniards were bound for New Orleans from Santa Fe in about 1797. The Spaniards dumped their gold in a slough during the fight. A white oak tree with a limb sagging down pointed to the location. To mark the tree, two plugs were cut out of the tree and pegged.

Later (in the 1860s), a man from New Orleans arrived along Lee's Creek after Cherokees had been relocated to Indian Territory. He convinced several Cherokees to help him drain a slough. He told the Cherokees his father was a survivor of the Arapaho attack and gave him directions to the gold's location. The Cherokees became uncooperative and forced the survivor's son to leave the country.

Tom Hilton wrote a detailed article, "Treasure on Lee's Creek," in *Treasure World* about how he learned of the lost gold and his efforts to find the treasure. The Cherokee families in the area were descendants of the Cherokees who helped the survivor's son look for the treasure in the 1860s. Floods changed the channel of Lee's Creek, creating sloughs and islands, and covered parts of the old channel with sediment. One Cherokee who cut down trees in the area remembered the tree with the two plugs.

This is one of those stories where something happened in the past on Lee's Creek. There was likely some treasure hidden. Both Frenchmen and Spaniards could have been involved, as Louisiana had been part of both empires. If it was gold dust from mining in New Mexico or northern Mexico, then the bags would have turned to dust by now. The currents in Lee's Creek may have scattered it downstream, unless the slough was cut off and buried by silt in situ. If it was bullion or partly bullion, it would be easier to locate.

Phillip Usray's Treasure Box

Cherokee Phillip Usray (Ussery) had a place in the Cherokee Hills, just east of or near Sallisaw. Usray tried to remain neutral during the Civil War as savage warfare raged all around him between Cherokees on both sides. Livestock on farms was taken by both the Confederate and Union forces if the owners did not sell it to them. Usray sold his horses and mules to the Union army and returned home with the gold payment.

Phillip Usray's grandson George recounted watching his grandfather get a tin box, into which he put the gold, a gold watch and his wife's jewelry. He then wrapped the tin box in sheepskin. He retrieved a shovel from the barn and took his young grandson to a nearby spring. He told his grandson to remain at the spring while he buried the tin box for safekeeping.

Not long afterward, Phillip Usray returned without the tin box, and they went to his home. That evening, Usray and his grandson had a quiet evening meal. There was a loud knock at the door and an angry man outside yelled, "Open up this door!" Phillip Usray quickly helped

George into a hiding place under the floor. The door was kicked in by three masked robbers. The robbers entered, demanding Usray turn over his gold to them or die. It is likely the robbers were soldiers or friends of soldiers at the Union post where he sold his livestock. Usray refused to tell them anything. The three robbers took Phillip Usray outside to a tree. They put a noose around the old man's neck and looped it over a tree limb. Repeatedly, they pulled Usray off the ground enough to start him choking and gasping. He still would not reveal its location.

All the while, his grandson George was under the house, listening in fear. Usray was savagely beaten and still refused to disclose his treasure's location. Finally, he was stabbed to death. His body was left suspended in midair.

After the robbers left, the little boy crawled from underneath the house and ran three miles to a nearby house where his uncle Tobe Usray lived. Tobe Usray and others came to Phillip Usray's place and found him dead. In spite of a lot of searching, the treasure has reportedly never been found.

Pretty Boy Floyd Treasure

Outlaw Charles "Pretty Boy" Floyd was supposed to have hidden some of his loot near Sallisaw or in the Cookston Hills. Floyd and his associates robbed banks and people throughout Oklahoma in 1931 and 1932. He was killed by FBI agents and lawmen near East Liverpool, Ohio, on October 22, 1934.

STEPHENS COUNTY

Spanish Treasure

A Spanish treasure may have been cached on Mud Creek.

TILLMAN COUNTY

Bank Robbery Loot

Loot from a Wichita Falls, Texas bank robbery was reportedly hidden on the Climers Ranch southwest of Grandfield.

Otter Creek Loot

See Kiowa County.

Wagon Train Massacre Treasure

A wagon train was massacred south of Frederick. A treasure from the wagon train may have been buried near Fort Augar (Camp Augar), which was established in 1871 to provide protection from hostile Indian attacks.

TULSA COUNTY

Dalton Gang $9,000 Cache

See Nowata County.

Dalton Hideouts

The Dalton Caves are located along Shell Creek, north of Sand Springs, and were used by the Dalton Gang. The Dalton Gang also used a farm near Sand Springs owned by Jack Wimberley as a hideout. When Emmett Dalton came to the Tulsa and Sand Springs area after being released from prison, some thought he recovered some buried loot. Three mysterious holes were found about three miles east of the Dalton Caves then.

Ed Lockhart Loot

Ed Lockhart was an outlaw whose gang stole as much as $500,000 from 1921 until his death on March 27, 1924. He robbed banks in Arkansas and Oklahoma. He was part of a gang that included Henry Starr, Charlie Brackett and Rufus Rollen, and they robbed a Harrison, Arkansas bank in 1921. In Oklahoma, he robbed banks in Gore, Mazie, Hulbert, Park Hill, Gentry, Bethany and perhaps thirteen other towns. He also robbed jewelry stores, post offices and railroads. The area he roamed and likely cached some of his loot in was Afton, Jay, Commerce and Pawhuska. Lockhart had been arrested several times a few days after a robbery, but no loot was ever found on him.

Lawmen knew he had stashed some loot from a Gore bank when he was arrested in Sallisaw. They tried to get him to cooperate to recover the loot. Lockhart was tried, sentenced and convicted to twenty years in prison. He was granted leave from prison after four months. He robbed more banks. He may have been granted leave so lawmen could trace down where he hid his loot.

Lockhart was quickly tracked down to a barn near Jay, where officers finally arrested him again after watching to see if he recovered any of his loot. They searched the barn and found no loot. Lockhart was held in the Delaware County Jail in Jay for two days before five members of his gang broke him out. Lockhart hid for a couple of months.

A tip caused a posse to surround a farm on March 27, 1924, outside of Sperry. The posse included Tulsa County Sheriff Bob Standford and a few men, including Mont Grady, a McAlester prison guard. Lockhart was ordered to come out by Grady, who knocked on the door while the posse covered him. Lockhart rushed out and fired a few shots as Grady tackled him. Grady lost his pistol, which Lockhart put into his own coat pocket. Lockhart used Grady as a shield, holding his gun against Grady's body. Grady managed to put a hand into Lockhart's pocket and pull the trigger on his pistol now pointed at Lockhart. Lockhart died on the spot.

It is likely that most of Lockhart's loot was in currency rather than coins. Since there were other gang members in the robberies, there were splits of the loot. Nevertheless, some of Ed Lockhart's loot probably remains hidden somewhere.

Lookout Mountain Treasure

A treasure was supposed to have been hidden on Lookout Mountain, near Thirty-First Street in West Tulsa. An Indian looking for the gold in the 1930s came to Tulsa and, with refinery worker Ray Vance, looked for a cave said to contain gold supposedly left by the Spanish or outlaws. After the Indian left, Vance spent a lot of time searching for the cave. He found what appeared to be a filled-in cave and began digging it out. One night, he hit hard rock at about six feet of depth. He thought he needed explosives to remove it. The next day when he returned, he found it was just a large hard rock and someone had removed it. In the dirt below, it looked like impressions of about fifteen metal bars that had been taken from the hole.

Lookout Mountain. *Author's photo.*

Lost City area. *Author's photo.*

Lost City Cache

The James Gang (Frank James) was said to have hidden $88,000 in cash wrapped in leather that was put in a small crevice at Lost City, an area about two to three miles southeast of Sand Springs. It contains some sandstone rock shelters and small caves along with ravines and small creeks. It is adjacent to the south road that runs along the Arkansas River called Avery Drive. An old rifle with the inscribed name of "G. Dalton" was said to have been found in one of the caves in Lost City. There is speculation that the name is Grat Dalton, one of the Dalton brothers who was an outlaw.

Tulsa Spanish Treasure

A Spanish party with gold was reportedly chased by Indians to a spring just south of present downtown Tulsa along the east bank of the Arkansas River. This spring was located just south of an old Indian trail that led to a ford across the Arkansas River. This ford originally was called Gano's Crossing after Confederate General Richard M. Gano, who, with Confederate Cherokee General Stand Watie, had forded the Arkansas River there with more than one hundred captured Union wagons from the Second Battle of Cabin Creek in 1864.

The ford was popular, as the bottom of the Arkansas River was an outcrop of checkerboard limestone, which wagons and horses could generally cross safely at low water. Most of the Arkansas River had a very sandy bottom, which was difficult to cross without a boat. The checkerboard limestone looks like a checkerboard of squares due to the natural jointing. Today, the site of the ford is roughly where the Eleventh Street Bridge crosses the Arkansas River. The Eleventh Street Bridge is where the Mother Road, or old U.S. 66, crossed the Arkansas River.

Tulsa was established in 1828 as Talise or Tulsey Town at this ford. Most of Tulsa then was on high ground north of Fifteenth Street, with the Creek Tribal Council grounds located at Eleventh Street and South Cheyenne Street.

These Spaniards supposedly hid their gold near the spring and disappeared. Evidently, some escaped death. In 1904, a man called Farley arrived at the small agricultural town of Tulsa, Creek Nation, with a map said to be eighteen inches by eighteen inches that had the location of the gold based on the Arkansas River ford, a creek, a big cottonwood tree and a spring. There

Arkansas River at Eleventh Street. *Author's photo.*

were fewer than one thousand people in the area then. Farley needed help in his search, so he talked local Creek citizen W. "Bill" S. Foreman (Foresman) into helping him search for the gold.

The January 1, 1933 edition of the *Tulsa World* published an article "Legend Says Gold Lies Beneath Tulsa Soil," which recounted Foreman's tale of searching for this lost Spanish treasure in Tulsa. They found cottonwood trees along the river, including a very old one that they believed to have markings carved on the tree trunk that were key to locating the gold. They could not read the markings and thought the original tree had been cut down. They found a nearby spring about nine feet in diameter and three feet deep. Water from the spring went into the sandy Arkansas River. Using metal rods, they probed sand around the spring but hit nothing solid. They thought maybe the gold had been hidden on the spring's edge.

They used a divining rod to search. They dug a ditch to drain the spring of water so they could dig along and in the spring. The two men had a couple of divining rod reactions in the spring. Each time they dug, they hit metal objects that turned out to be old rusty shovels. As they dug in the spring, the water influx and moving sand made it impossible to dig deeper.

When the article appeared in 1933, the spring had been filled in and may have been located a block or so south of Eleventh Street and east of Riverside Parkway (Riverside Drive). The spring was likely at the base of the river terrace, which has been cut to build houses and apartments. The cut material from the terrace was likely placed on the riverside to elevate what is now Riverside Parkway and River Parks. The creek had been moved and is a storm drain.

Turkey Mountain Civil War Treasure

In September 1902, long after the Civil War ended, an ex-soldier returned to Red Fork (West Tulsa). He employed livery stable driver Bill Barnett to take him to nearby Turkey Mountain. There he recovered an old kettle with gold coins he had buried during the Civil War. The kettle with the gold coins had been buried on Turkey Mountain, with the marker being a rock with the number "64" carved on it. He used a compass and measuring tape to relocate his cache. Turkey Mountain is now a nature park. The man claimed he knew of other treasures in the area and planned to search for them.

Turkey Mountain. *Author's photo.*

Younger Gang Arkansas River Loot

Cole Younger was rumored to have hidden $63,000 on the south side of the Arkansas River about one mile east of the Sand Springs bridge. "Scout" Younger claimed to be Cole Younger's cousin. According to an April 18, 1917 edition of the *Oklahoma Leader*, Scout Younger led a group looking for Cole Younger's treasure. This is the same area as the Lost City Cache discussed previously.

WAGONER COUNTY

Three Forks Found Treasure

Spanish coins were found before 1940 in the Three Forks area on the Verdigris River and Arkansas River junction. The Three Forks area was a key location for trading posts in the Indian nations due to its strategic location near the junction of the Grand River, Arkansas River and Verdigris River. One trading post was Wigwam Neosho, which was run by Sam Houston. Sam Houston then went to settle in Texas, became the Texian general who defeated Mexican General Santa Anna at the Battle of San Jacinto and became a Republic of Texas president. In 1965, a Tulsa couple found fifty-one twenty-dollar gold pieces and other relics in the Three Forks area. Some old trading posts were excavated by archaeologists during the construction of the Arkansas Navigation Project by the U.S. Army Corps of Engineers.

WASHINGTON COUNTY

Al Spencer Gang Loot

Albert "Al" Spencer and his gang robbed the Katy (Missouri, Kansas and Texas) Railroad train at Okesa of $20,000 in cash and bonds ($65 in cash and $20,000 in liberty bonds) on August 20, 1923. This may have been the last Oklahoma train robbery.

Spencer was ambushed by thirteen lawmen, including U.S. Marshal Alva McDonald, Kansas City postal inspector Jack Adamson, Bartlesville Chief of Police L.A. Gaston, Chief Deputy Marshal Duke Stalling, Indian agent officer William Crow, postal inspector W.W. Haynes, Katy detective

Joe Palmer, operative Rob Taylor, Oklahoma City cop Luther Bishop, Oklahoma City police Lieutenant Harry Wolf, Oklahoma City prosecutor C.F. Robb and federal agent Ed Robinson.

Al Spencer had just crossed a bridge near Nowata while taking the bonds to someone who would convert them to cash. The lawmen were on both sides of the road in a chilly drizzle. After someone yelled "Hands up!" Spencer was said to have fired his rifle at the lawmen. The lawmen fired back, with at least three bullets hitting Spencer near his heart.

Some posse members had personal grudges against Al Spencer. Gaston believed his house had been shot up by the Spencer Gang. One man's son was murdered during a post office robbery in Pawhuska a few months previously by the Spencer Gang.

The *Pawhuska Daily Capitol* on September 17, 1923, reported Al Spencer had $10,000 in $1,000 bonds in his left hand and his Winchester in his right hand. Since Spencer had just fired a rifle shot as the waiting lawmen shot and killed him, this description is likely literary license.

The $10,000 in bonds were recovered from his body. There was another $10,000 in bonds not accounted for, which may have been hidden by him or was in the hands of other gang members. Another story claimed that a shovel with dirt on it was said to have been found about fifty yards from his body, leading many to believe the bonds were buried by him just before he was killed. Another variation of this tale indicated the Spencer Gang may have hidden loot in woods about two miles southwest of Caney, Kansas, in Washington County, Oklahoma, near the Kansas-Oklahoma border.

WASHITA COUNTY

Old Mexican Coins Found

Seven old human skeletons and forty-nine Mexican coins dated 1846–49, along with Mexican-style gear, were found near Cloud Chief in several locations by prospectors looking for gold over a few months in 1895, as reported in the *Cloud Chief Herald-Sentinel*. These coins may have been from people coming from California or Mexico during the gold rush period who were attacked and killed by Indians.

Soldier Treasure

See Custer County.

Turkey Creek Treasure

A Spanish or miners' treasure of gold bars may have been hidden on Turkey Creek near Canute. There are stories of an old Mexican town of Cascorillo being located about two to three miles southwest of Canute. Steve Wilson wrote about this site in his book and in an article called "Cascorillo" in *Treasure World* magazine.

UNKNOWN COUNTY

Dick Estes Loot

In 1902, Dick Estes robbed a jeweler in Denver, Colorado, of about $40,000 in jewelry and watches along with $20,000 in gold coins. Estes fled to Oklahoma Territory to his hideout in the Wichita Mountains on Panther Creek. He hid the bulk of his loot and kept only enough for living expenses. One story reported that a cedar tree about ten paces west of a dugout was key to locating his burial site. Dick Estes left the area, was arrested, escaped for two years, was again arrested and spent his remaining days in jail. He may never have made it back to retrieve his loot. Jim Wilkerson claimed Estes told him about the treasure location when he traded the information for a horse and saddle when Estes was on the run. Steve Wilson's book documents this tale.

Found Silver Ingots

In October 1971, the Associated Press reported several silver ingots with a cross and crown imbedded on them were found by Bill Ferrel and Don Cagle. The original story was published in the *Lawton Constitution* and also reprinted in the *Lubbock Avalanche-Journal* on October 14, 1971. Bill Ferrel wrote an article about the find called "Spanish Silver Found in Oklahoma" for the December 1972 edition of *Western Treasures*. Ferrel claimed the location was

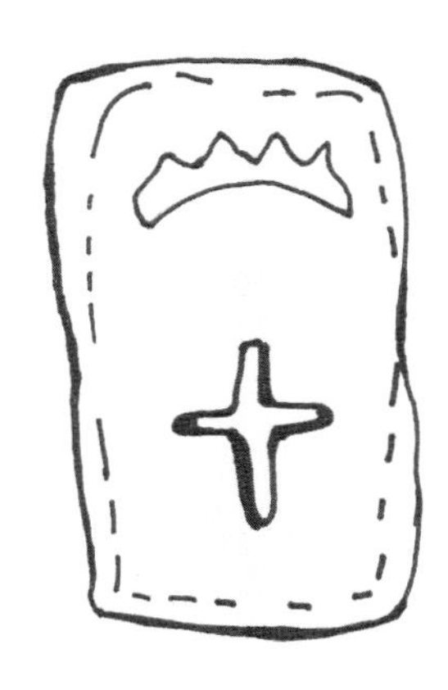

Silver ingot drawing. *Author's photo*.

not in the Wichita Mountains but one hundred miles away from Lawton. Some sources indicate it was found in a cave west of Meers. Ferrel and Cagle used an ancient map to find the treasure in a cave after a fifteen-year search after finding the original marker on the map. The map was said to have had the year "1635" on it. They refused to give the location of the cave, which was six feet wide and seven feet tall and could not be seen until you were in front of it. It was in a narrow ravine. They had to walk ninety feet up a narrow passage. They dug two feet of fill and found at least two silver ingots that assayed at 87 percent silver and clay molds where the ingots were made.

Gold Nuggets

A man said he took refuge in a cavern-like low area that contained gold nuggets in the Wichita Mountains while hiding from Indians. He did not return to the area.

Mexican Gold Vein

A gold vein was reportedly found by a Mexican in the western Wichita Mountains. The man who found it operated out of Vernon, Texas (Downing's Line Camp).

CHAPTER 2

WICHITA MOUNTAINS

The Wichita Mountains tower above southwestern Oklahoma's rolling prairie like supernatural guardians of lost mines and treasure. The Wichita Mountains were formed more than 500 million years ago by molten rock rising from the Earth's crust on a northwest to southeast trend that runs through Greer, Jackson, Kiowa and Comanche Counties. The Wichita Mountains are made of granite, gabbro, breccia and diabase dikes. These ancient rocks were covered by salty oceans for millions of years. Finally, these rocks were all uplifted and eroded for more millions of years until the igneous rock was finally exposed at the surface where we see it today. Igneous rocks are often a great place to look for gold, silver and other minerals. Mineral deposits are often found along faulted and fractured rock. Deeply buried rock contained high-temperature, mineral-rich fluids that moved through faults and fractures and sometimes deposited valuable minerals in them.

The Wichita Mountains contain Devil's Canyon, Treasure Lake, Cache Creek and Cutthroat Gap, the names of which all give clues to this area's past. Spanish and French explorers encountered Indians from many tribes in the mountains and surrounding plains and left tales of lost mines and buried gold and silver. Legends of Spanish mining range from the 1600s to 1820. What is called the Old Spanish Trail ran from Santa Fe to Nacogdoches, Texas, and then to New Orleans through the Wichita Mountains. The Spanish called the Wichita Mountains the Sierra Jumanos. In 1629, Padre Juan de Salas came from Santa Fe to convert Native Americans in the area but was not successful in converting them to Christianity or finding gold. Captain Don Diego del Castillo led an expedition into the Wichita Mountains in about 1650 to search for gold and silver. His party reportedly spent six months looking for riches without much success.

Many treasure tales take place north of Treasure Lake near Mount Pinchot in the Charon's Gardens wilderness area. In 1901, a gold rush started in the Wichita Mountains when the U.S. government dissolved the Kiowa-Comanche-Apache Indian reservation and opened the area up for public mining claims. The igneous rocks in the Wichita Mountains are similar to other mineral-bearing areas that have been extremely productive. Miners and geologists believed significant gold and mineral deposits were present in the Wichita Mountains. Thousands of prospectors and miners staked mining claims and did some mining. Only a couple of bars of copper and silver with a tiny amount of gold were ever refined from their mining efforts. By 1907, the gold rush was bust, with thousands of shallow prospects examined. However, platinum and other minerals could exist at deeper depths than these miners reached.

The majority of the eastern Wichita Mountains are part of the U.S. Fish and Wildlife Service's Wichita Mountains Wildlife Refuge. The wildlife refuge contains herds of buffalo, elk and longhorn cattle and is a fun place

Wichita mineral outcrop. *Author's photo.*

Old mine dump in the Wichita Mountains. *Author's photo.*

to visit wildlife. Disturbing and removing anything is prohibited. A portion of the eastern Wichita Mountains and the area to the south between Lawton and the mountains is mostly in the Fort Sill Military Reservation and has restricted access. Much of the western Wichita Mountains is accessible with the surface owner's permission. Silver was found near Mangum, Greer County. Old mine shafts are also located near Hobart, Kiowa County, and Cache, Comanche County. Comanche County and Kiowa County contain the Wichita Mountains and have many lost treasure and lost mine stories.

CHAPTER 3

TRADERS AND TRAVELERS

After the Europeans came to North America, what is known as Oklahoma was a borderland as mostly part of French Louisiana with parts of the area claimed by Spain. The area in western Oklahoma was inhabited by Plains Indians such as the Comanches, Kiowas and Wichitas, while eastern Oklahoma was inhabited by such tribes as the Osage and Caddo. French traders established trading posts with the Indian tribes at a number of locations in Oklahoma. The French also looked for precious mineral deposits, and several legends of lost mines come from this period.

In 1762, under the Treaty of Fontainebleau, France turned Louisiana over to Spain at the end of the Seven Years' War. After a rebellion by the French population against Spain in 1767, Spain managed to completely take over all of Louisiana. Trade between Santa Fe, New Mexico, St. Louis and New Orleans occurred during this time. Spanish trails went through Oklahoma. A number of legends of lost Spanish gold and treasure are from this period.

In 1800, as part of the Treaty of San Ildefonso, Spain transferred Louisiana back to France. French possession of the territory was not immediate. Napoleon sold Louisiana to the United States in 1803 in what became the Louisiana Purchase, which included most of present Oklahoma.

After a long series of revolutions, Mexico became an independent country from Spain in 1821. Overland trade developed between Mexican Santa Fe and St. Louis merchants along what became the Santa Fe Trail. The Cimarron Cutoff on the Santa Fe Trail cut through Cimarron County. Several lost treasures are associated with the Cimarron Cutoff.

Some members of the Five Civilized Tribes migrated to current areas of Oklahoma, Texas and Arkansas. The Indian Removal Act of 1830 forced most members of the Five Civilized Tribes onto lands in present eastern and central Oklahoma on lands formerly occupied by other tribes.

With the discovery of gold in California in 1848, thousands of gold seekers headed down the California Road from Fort Smith, Arkansas, through the Indian nations in present Oklahoma. Several treasures were said to have been cached in Kay, Nowata, Okfuskee, Osage and Washington Counties by those returning from gold fields in California, Colorado or Montana.

The Texas Road (Military Road, Shawnee Trail) from Fort Scott, Kansas, to Colbert's Ferry was also used to move cattle from Texas to Kansas and Missouri. The Chisholm Trail and Western Trail were also used to move cattle to market in Kansas. Several lost treasures were associated with these trails.

Railroads were built through Oklahoma and carried people, cargo and money. Outlaws robbed a number of trains, as indicated by stories of the Dalton Gang, Doolin-Dalton Gang and other outlaw gangs that infested the area.

Oklahoma is still a crossroads of trade and transportation, connecting the West and East Coasts of the United States as well northern and southern areas.

Chapter 4

KNIGHTS OF THE GOLDEN CIRCLE

The Knights of the Golden Circle (KGC) was a secret society formed before the American Civil War to extend slave states into Latin America and to form a slaveholding southern government. This was a secret society related to the rites and organizational structure of the Masons, which were also related to the Knights Templar. What is often called the KGC was a number of different groups or secret cells. In 1854, the KGC was organized as a consolidation of various southern rights clubs and was headquartered in Cincinnati, Ohio. Many believe its members played a key role in starting the Civil War. Many pro-KGC or antiwar people were called Copperheads, due to their symbol of an Indian head copper penny, which represented American liberty. The Confederate Secret Service used the KGC members and Copperheads as spies and agents.

KGC members were active in bank and Union payroll robberies, started unrest in Chicago to free Confederate prisoners at Camp Douglas and caused draft riots and set fires in New York City in 1864. They also set fires to Union steamboats and warehouses.

Due to the secret nature of the KGC, little evidence has been found about it or how it operated clandestinely. Confederate Secret Service records were destroyed as the Civil War ended. This prevented the arrests and conviction of KGC members and Confederate spies and protected Confederate sympathizers in powerful positions. Most of the secret activities of the KGC and Confederate Secret Service were never written down.

Albert Pike. *Library of Congress.*

One well-known key member of the KGC is Albert Pike, who was an Arkansas attorney and newspaperman who lived in Little Rock. Pike served in the Mexican War along with many others, such as Jefferson Davis, who became leaders of the Confederacy. In 1859, Pike was elected sovereign grand commander of the Scottish Rite Masons. During the Civil War, he was a Confederate Indian agent to tribes in the Indian nations and was a Confederate brigadier general who commanded an Indian brigade.

He resigned his commission in 1862 over repeated disputes with other Confederate generals. Pike was the mastermind behind Scottish Rite Masonic rituals and their organization in the United States. Albert Pike wrote *Morals and Dogma of the Ancient and Accepted Scottish Rite of Freemasonry*, which is the classic work on the Scottish Rite organization. After the Civil War, Albert Pike lived in Washington, D.C. From the Masonic Lodge there, Pike directed the Masons until he died in 1891. Most Masonic lodges in the United States exhibit busts of Pike's head and information on him. Pike traveled extensively directing the Masonic movement and possibly on KGC business after the Civil War. Stand Watie, the Confederate Cherokee general, and other Cherokees were also said to have been members of the KGC.

The KGC and other pro-KGC groups were said to have accumulated large sums of currency, gold and silver during and after the Civil War. The KGC raised funds from member contributions. During the Civil War, KGC money may have been acquired through Union payroll robberies, bank robberies, sale of cotton and other means. Confederate Secret Service agents in Canada and the North funneled large sums of cash to Copperheads to buy guns and ammunition. Confederate Secret Service funds were never accounted for and just disappeared. Some believe these monies were hidden to support further rebellion and continue the Lost Cause. The KGC was said to have used geometric systems to note where its buried treasure was hidden. Markers on the ground were tied to maps. There were also codes that only members of the KGC could decipher. The Confederate Secret Service, the Copperheads, the KGC and affiliated organizations used ciphers and secret writing.

After the Civil War, some ex-Confederates, who often were members of the KGC or similar organizations, refused to admit defeat. These hardcore Confederates left the United States and settled in England, Mexico and Brazil. Most KGC members, like Jesse James, stayed in the United States. Some followed an outlaw and anti-government path of life. Jesse James and his band robbed many trains and banks and may have left treasure in Arkansas, Kansas, Missouri and Oklahoma. Many of the treasures attributed to the KGC are outlaw caches.

In Oklahoma, several small coin caches, including gold coins, have been found that some say were part of KGC treasure caches. Bob Brewer (coauthor of *Rebel Gold/Shadow of the Sentinel*) spent many years researching and interpreting maps, markers and symbols looking for KGC treasure.

The Wapanucka treasure caches were buried long after the Civil War, based on the coin dates. These treasures were found based on complex treasure maps from Jesse James and the James Gang. Treasure hunter Joe Hunter had acquired maps and found money and associated artifacts in the 1930s and 1940s that were likely from the Jesse James Gang. There is some controversy over the Wapanucka find, and other buried Jesse James Gang or KGC treasure might be nearby. Based on symbols that some have found on the ground, some believe many KGC treasures were hidden. There were said to be KGC and associated anti-government cells all over the United States. For more information, see Comanche County, "James Gang $2 Million Cache and Other Caches"; Jefferson County, "Addington Treasure"; and Johnson County, "Wapanucka Treasures."

Chapter 5

OUTLAWS AND THEIR LOOT

Information on Oklahoma outlaws is often hard to verify, as they often used many aliases, moved around a lot and seldom told the truth. Outlaws were not good people. They paid cash to poor farmers and ranchers to hide them from authorities and to keep quiet. Much information has been accumulated on famous outlaws since the 1950s, when interest in the Old West surged in movies, books and magazines. There is a lot of conflicting information that I have tried to sort through.

Outlaws and guerrilla gangs committed crimes and murders during the Civil War. The Cherokee Nation, Creek Nation and other Indian nations were depopulated as the Civil War divided tribal members and families. Large amounts of money were cached and never recovered due to the fears of robbery. Quantrill's Confederate guerrillas (which included the James brothers and Younger brothers, as well as Belle Starr's future husband) passed through the Indian nations during the Civil War. Many surviving members of Quantrill's guerrillas became outlaws after the Civil War after having learned gunfighting and robbery skills.

Before statehood, Oklahoma was composed of various Indian nations and reservations in addition to unassigned lands with little law enforcement except for U.S. marshals out of Fort Smith, Arkansas, and tribal lawmen. Tribal lawmen only had jurisdiction over Native Americans from their tribe. Sometimes the U.S. military got involved in preserving law and order. During the Civil War and thereafter, bands of outlaws were formed and raided roads and farms in Oklahoma. The Reynolds Gang and Coe Gang raided the

Cimarron Cutoff in western Oklahoma. For more information on this, see Cimarron County, "Reynolds Gang Treasures" and "Robbers Roost."

One of the most prolific outlaw gangs was the James Gang, which was led by Jesse James and his brother Frank and contained members of the Younger Gang and other outlaws. Frank Tripett's book on Jesse James tabulated $263,278 in James Gang robberies from 1866 until 1881 from twenty train, bank and stagecoach robberies. The members of the James Gang individually or in smaller groups likely stole much more money. Since Oklahoma was sparsely settled and contained little law enforcement, it became a favorite hideout of outlaws between the Civil War and statehood in 1907.

Jesse James was killed on April 3, 1882, by Robert Ford in St. Joseph, Missouri. Ford claimed a $10,000 reward but was paid only a small portion of it. Frank James was a fugitive for a long time. He negotiated terms of surrender to authorities and was tried for only a few robberies and a murder in Missouri. Due to a combination of politics, Reconstruction animosities and legal tricks, he was able to avoid conviction and never spent any time in prison, although he was jailed several times. Frank James bought a farm near Fletcher, Oklahoma, and reportedly found several caches of James Gang treasures nearby, but not all of them. See Caddo County, "Frank James Treasure"; Comanche County, "James Gang $2 Million Cache and Other Caches"; Jefferson County, "Addington Treasure"; and Johnson County, "Wapanucka Treasures."

In the 1880s through Oklahoma statehood, cattle raising syndicates leased land for cattle grazing and hired cowboys with little pay who desired an outdoors adventurous life. A number of these cowboys became outlaws and formed the Dalton Gang, Doolin-Dalton Gang and other noted outlaw gangs. These cowboys-turned-outlaws knew the country and evaded lawmen who were less skilled in the wild. The outlaws robbed trains and individuals as well as banks. See Haskell County, "Belle Starr Treasures"; Johnson County, "Bill Cook's Lost Loot"; Le Flore County, "Henry Starr Treasures"; Nowata County, "Dalton Gang's $9,000 Cache"; Payne County, "Doolin-Dalton Gang's Ingalls Area"; and Tulsa County, "Lost City Cache" and "Younger Gang Arkansas River Loot."

Ed Lockhart, Al Spencer and Al Jennings were some of the last outlaws of an era that changed from robbing banks by horseback to using automobiles. See Tulsa County, "Ed Lockhart Loot" and Washington County, "Al Spencer Gang Loot."

Charles Fletcher Taylor, Jesse James and Frank James. *Missouri Historical Society.*

Regarding outlaw loot that was buried and hidden, it was most likely the gold and silver coins that were too heavy to carry on a horse when a posse was chasing after the outlaws. After a robbery, the outlaws had to split up the loot, and then they would often bury it. When hard-pressed by a posse on horseback, outlaws often hid the heavy coins not far from the robbery site and then split into different directions to confuse the posse. The outlaws usually rode better horses than the posse and so usually had an edge when escaping. Often, the outlaws had fresh horses staked along their escape route so they could outpace the posses. Individual outlaws seem to have often had a number of small caches of loot to draw on over time.

The finds of small caches of coins near Wapanucka based on maps said to have been made by Jesse James indicate that having a number of caches was common. The outlaws could not deposit their loot in banks, so they would have to hide some of it for a rainy day when they needed cash between robberies. With the development of roads, motor cars, telegraph lines and telephone lines connecting towns, it became hard for outlaws to escape. Many outlaw gang members died with their boots on and took the locations of their caches with them to the grave. Some buried treasure has been found over the years, and much likely remains to be found.

Chapter 6

THE INDIAN NATIONS

Before the Civil War, Indian nations covered much of Oklahoma. The Indian nations were mostly organized into Oklahoma Territory and Indian Territory before the state of Oklahoma was created in 1907. Many Indian reservations were abolished and open for settlement, but the Five Civilized Tribes lands remained under some tribal authority.

The Cherokee Nation in Oklahoma covers Adair, Cherokee, Craig, Delaware, Mayes, Nowata, Rogers, Sequoyah and Washington Counties, as well as part of MacIntosh, Muskogee, Ottawa and Tulsa Counties. Cherokee lands also at one time included the Cherokee strip in present Kansas, the Cherokee Outlet and Cherokee Neutral Lands. The Cherokee Nation has many tales of lost family caches, hidden outlaw treasure and lost mines. There are several stories of lost Cherokee Nation government treasure in the Tahlequah area. The Dalton Gang was supposed to have buried a number of treasures in the Cherokee Nation area.

The Muskogee Creek Nation covers Creek, Okfuskee and Okmulgee Counties, as well as parts of Hughes, McIntosh, Muskogee, Tulsa and Wagoner Counties. Opothleyahola's Creek Nation treasure in McIntosh County or Payne County is one of the most interesting treasures in Oklahoma. A number of other Civil War caches are also located in the Muskogee Creek Nation.

The Choctaw Nation covers Atoka, Choctaw, Haskell, Latimer, Le Flore, McCurtain and Pushmataha Counties, as well as parts of Bryan, Coal, Johnson, Pontotoc and Stephens Counties. Belle Starr's Treasure at

Younger's Bend is another outlaw story with lost treasure. A number of lost mines were claimed to be located in the rugged mountains and hills of southeast Oklahoma.

The Chickasaw Nation covers Carter, Garvin, Love, Marshall, McLain, Murray and parts of Bryan, Coal, Grady, Jefferson, Johnson and Pontotoc Counties. The James Gang, outlaw Bill Cook and other outlaw treasures are located in the Chickasaw Nation. Several small caches likely to belong to members of the James Gang have reportedly been recovered near Wapanucka.

The Seminole Nation covers Seminole County and contains stories of lost and found treasure.

The Osage Reservation was created from what had been previously known as part of the Cherokee Outlet. Osages were required to move there from reservations in Kansas. Osage County covers the Osage Reservation. Numerous outlaws used this area as their hideouts, and a number of treasures are detailed in the Osage County listing of lost treasure. "Goldie's Lost Gold" is one of the most interesting and possibly richest lost treasure tale.

The Comanche Nation covers all or parts of Caddo, Comanche, Cotton, Grady, Kiowa, Stephens and Tillman Counties. The Wichita Mountains that cover parts of this area abound with many tales of lost mines and lost treasure, including a lost Spanish mining district. Jesse James and his gang have a number of lost loot stories, with some loot recovered over the years. The $2 million Jesse James Loot is supposed to be in the Keechi Hills or Wichita Mountains.

Other lost treasures are associated with the Otoe Reservation and other Indian lands in northeastern Oklahoma.

CHAPTER 7

SHIPWRECKS

Today, the Arkansas River Navigation System conveys barges to and from the Port of Catoosa, Oklahoma, on the Verdigris River through locks and dams on the Arkansas River to the Mississippi River. In the early to late 1800s, steamboats traveled the winding Arkansas River from the Mississippi River to Fort Gibson, Cherokee Nation. These early steamboats ranged in size from 75 to 150 tons and were shallow-bottomed vessels.

Fort Gibson, Cherokee Nation, was the U.S. fort on the Grand River that had a landing. In 1828, the steamboat *Facility* was a 117-ton vessel that brought 780 Creeks up the Verdigris River and returned downstream with a cargo of pelts, hides and about five hundred barrels of pecans. The navigation season ranged from December to July, when rains on the Great Plains and Ozark Mountains caused river depths to be high enough for small steamboats to travel on the Arkansas River

Some landings from the limit of navigation to Fort Smith, Arkansas, were Fort Gibson (1824–59 U.S. military post and 1861–90 Confederate, Union and U.S. military post), Creek Agency Landing (near Muskogee), Bayou Menard, Green Leaf, Webbers Falls (in 1807 it had a waterfall seven feet high and could only be passed in very high water), Illinois, Canadian (see McIntosh County, "Dr. John J. Hayes's Lost Gold"), Pheasant Bluff, Vian, Fort Coffee (U.S. military post established in 1834–43 and 1861–62) and Fort Smith (established in 1817).

One of the first steamboats to sink on the Arkansas River was the fifty-eight-ton *S.B. Spy*, which was snagged at the Devil's Race Ground on the Arkansas River in early 1833. The Devil's Race Ground was a series of shallow sand shoals that were a navigation hazard at low water about twenty miles downstream of Fort Gibson. In 1834, the one-hundred-ton *Little Rock* sank near Fort Smith on the Arkansas River with a cargo that included equipment for the dragoon regiment at Fort Gibson. The one-hundred-ton *Tom Bowline* hit a rock and sank at Webbers Falls. The *Tom Bowline* was raised and continued to navigate the Arkansas River for many years.

On April 18, 1839, the steamer *Bee* sank in the Grand River near Fort Gibson. The *Bee*'s furniture and boiler were salvaged from the wreck. Near Fort Smith, the *Harp Salem* hit a snag and sank in ten minutes. Nearby, the steamer *Indian* also sank.

During the Civil War, the sternwheel steamer *J.R. Williams* carried a valuable cargo worth $129,000 that included 150 barrels of flour, clothing, cloth, boots, sixteen thousand pounds of bacon shoulders, a ton of tea and 40 barrels of sugar. The *J.R. Williams* was bound from Fort Smith, Arkansas, for Fort Gibson, Cherokee Nation, to supply sixteen thousand hungry Union soldiers and civilian refugees. The *J.R. Williams* was normally used as a ferry at Fort Smith to move people and goods across the Arkansas River. It only had a twenty-six-man Union guard under Lieutenant Horace A.B. Cook of the Twelfth Kansas Cavalry Regiment. On June 15, 1864, the *J.R. Williams* passed by Pheasant Bluff (Pleasant Bluff), which was an elevated bluff on the south bank overlooking the Arkansas River near Tamaha about five miles below where the Canadian River entered the Arkansas River. A Confederate battery from Stand Watie's First Indian Brigade was on Pheasant Bluff and ambushed the steamboat. Three cannons under Lieutenant Forrester from Lee's Light Battery (Texas) were placed about one hundred yards apart on the bluff. Cannonballs landed in the vessel's upper works and splintered the pilot house, steam pipes and smokestacks. The *J.R. Williams* grounded on a sandbar on the north bank. Two men were killed and several wounded on the *J.R. Williams*. Most of the Union crew and guard escaped.

The Confederates floated the steamer onto a sandbar near the south bank. At least six Union soldiers were captured by Watie's men. Initially, the Confederates wanted to steam the *J.R. Williams* up the Arkansas River to the Canadian River and go up the Canadian River past Canadian landing in order to move the supplies closer to Confederate camps. This plan was abandoned, and the Confederates started unloading the badly needed supplies onto the sandbar. Lacking transportation, they could not move much. The Confederate Indian brigade's men took all the foodstuffs they could carry and headed back to their camps and families, who were desperately in need of food. The next morning, Union Colonel John R. Ritchie and part of his command arrived on the Arkansas River's north bank. They had marched from Macey's Salt Works and lime kiln located upstream at the mouth of the Illinois River after Union survivors from the *J.R. Williams* informed Colonel Ritchie of the Confederate attack. Union forces consisting of several cannons and the Second Kansas Colored Infantry Regiment were also on the south side of the Arkansas River, having advanced west from near Fort Smith. As they approached, the Union cannons began shelling the Confederates. Most of Watie's Brigade had already left with food for the camps, so Colonel Stand Watie and his mostly Cherokee Rebels retreated. On the evening of June 16, the Confederates set fire to the *J.R. Williams* and sent it floating downstream, where it sank.

Stand Watie. *Oklahoma Historical Society*.

By 1870, twenty steamboats cruised the Arkansas River until the railroads were built through the Indian nations. During the construction of the current navigation channel, several old steamboat anchors were recovered during dredging.

There was also some navigation on the Red River. In about 1850, a river steamer with a cargo of liquor, hardware and other goods was said to have sunk in the Red River near Pecan Point (Point aux Peconques) along the Spanish Trail. The location of the sinking was opposite Clarksville, Texas, downstream from the shoals that marked the upstream limits of navigation on the Red River at that time.

In 1893, the *Hennessey Clipper* newspaper wrote that a group of men—Joe Yates, John Grant, Mr. Wells, Tom Graham and another man—decided to look for the wreck sunk in 1850. It appears that the Red River had moved, and the wreck was under dry land. The men dug down through eighteen feet of sand. They were said to have recovered five wine casks, a few whiskey barrels, more than $1,000 in gold, china, a silver flask and an old sword.

Another shipwreck was discovered in 1991 by local landowners in the middle of the Red River when the river changed its channel and the water was low. In 1999, archaeologists were notified and came to examine the wreck. The Oklahoma Historical Society and archaeologists from the Institute of Nautical Archaeology from Texas A&M University investigated the wreck, which was under six feet of sediment. It was located a few miles below Fort Towson, Oklahoma. The recovery team retrieved hand trucks used for loading and unloading cargo, almonds, corn cobs, a barrel of pork and the engine and two paddle wheels of the ship. A helicopter removed the engine and paddle wheels from the middle of the Red River.

Investigation showed the shipwreck to be the steamer *Heroine*, which was built in 1832 and sunk in 1838 when it hit a tree stump in the Red River. The *Heroine* was a single-engine steamer about 140 feet long with a 26-foot-wide beam. It was going upstream bound for Fort Towson and Doaksville, Indian Territory, with a cargo. There are plans are to display the *Heroine*'s engine and paddle wheels at the Oklahoma History Center in Oklahoma City.

BIBLIOGRAPHY

Collections

Indian Pioneer History, Foreman Collection, Oklahoma Historical Society.

Government Document

U.S. Fish and Wildlife Service. *Wichita Mountains Wildlife Refuge*. Brochure, August 2013.

The War of the Rebellion: A Compilation of the Official Records of the Union and Confederate Armies. 128 vols. Washington, D.C.: Government Printing Office, 1880–1901.

Newspapers

Tulsa Daily World, 1931, 1932.

Books

Anderson, Dan, and Laurence Yadon. Edited by Robert Barr Smith. *100 Oklahoma Outlaws, Gangsters, and Lawmen, 1839–1939*. Gretna, LA: Pelican Publishing Company, 2010.

Cantrell, Mark Lea, and Mac Harris. *Kepis & Turkey Calls: An Anthology of the War Between the States in Indian Territory*. Oklahoma City: Western Heritage Books, Inc., 1982.

Cherokee County Historical Background. Tahlequah, OK, n.d.

Debo, Angie. *A History of the Creek Indians.* Norman: University of Oklahoma Press, 1979.

Dobie, J. Frank. *Coronado's Children.* New York: Literary Guild of America, 1931.

Foreman, Grant. *Marcy & the Gold Seekers*. Norman: University of Oklahoma Press, 1968.

Gaines, W. Craig. *Civil War Gold and Other Lost Treasure.* Revised Edition. N.p.: Amazon, 2017.

———. *The Confederate Cherokees: John Drew's Regiment of Mounted Rifles*. Baton Rouge: Louisiana State University Press, 1989.

———. *Encyclopedia of Civil War Shipwrecks.* Baton Rouge: Louisiana State University Press, 2008.

———. *Hispanic Lost Treasure of the Eastern United States*. N.p.: Amazon, 2019.

Getler, Warren, and Bob Brewer. *Rebel Gold.* New York: Simon & Schuster, 2005.

Gilbert, Dr. M. Charles. *The Wichita Mountains in Oklahoma: Their Story Through Time, Guidebook 39*. Norman: Oklahoma Geological Survey, 2014.

Hanes, Colonel Bailey C. *Bill Doolin, Outlaw O.T.* Norman: University of Oklahoma Press, 1968.

Henson, Michael Paul. *America's Lost Treasures*. South Bend, IN: Jayco Publishing Co., 1984.

Jameson, W.C. *Lost Mines and Buried Treasures of Oklahoma*. Henderson, TN: Goldminds Publishing LLC, 2013.

James, Thomas. *Three Years Among the Indians and Mexicans*. St. Louis: Missouri Historical Society, 1916. Repr. of 1846 publication.

Keehn, David C. *Knights of the Golden Circle: Secret Empire, Southern Secession, Civil War*. Baton Rouge: Louisiana State University Press, 2013.

Marx, Robert F. *Buried Treasure of the United States: How and Where to Locate Hidden Wealth*. New York: Bonanza Books, 1978.

Monaghan, Jay. *Civil War on the Western Border, 1854–1865*. New York: Bonanza Books, 1956.

Morris, John W. *Ghost Towns of Oklahoma*. Norman: University of Oklahoma, 1977.

Morris, John W., and Edwin C. McReynolds. *Historical Atlas of Oklahoma*. Norman: University of Oklahoma, 1971.

Patterson, Richard. *Historical Atlas of the Outlaw West.* Boulder, CO: Johnson Books, 1993.

Penfield, Thomas. *Buried Treasure in the U.S. and Where to Find It.* New York: Grosset & Dunlap, 1969.

Phillips, Paul Chester. *The Fur Trade.* Vol. 2. Norman: University of Oklahoma Press, 1967.

Price, Jonathan D. *The Wichita Mountains, Oklahoma: A Tour of Eocambrian Rifting and Permian Erosion, Field Guide for the 2015 AAPG Southwest Section Field Trip.* April 11, 2015.

Rascoe, Jesse (penname for Ed Bartholomew). *Oklahoma Treasures Lost and Found.* Fort Davis, TX: Frontier Book Co., 1971.

Schurmacher, Emile C. *Lost Treasures and How to Find Them!* New York: Paperback Library (Coronet Communications), 1968.

Settle, William A., Jr. *Jesse James Was His Name.* Lincoln: University of Nebraska Press, 1977.

Shirley, Glenn. *Henry Starr: Last of the Real Badmen.* New York: David McKay Company, Inc., 1965.

———. *Law West of Fort Smith: A History of Frontier Justice in the Indian Territory, 1834–1896.* Lincoln: University of Nebraska Press, 1968.

Terry, Thomas P. *United States Treasure Map Atlas.* La Crosse, WI: Specialty Publishing Company, 1981.

Triplett, Frank. *The Life, Times & Treacherous Death of Jesse James.* Reprint of 1882 edition. Stamford, CT: Longmeadow Press, 1992.

Turpin, Robert F. *Outlaw Bill Cook's Buried Gold.* Kindle edition, 2014.

Wilson, Steve. *Oklahoma Treasure and Treasure Tales.* Norman: University of Oklahoma Press, 1980.

Wright, Muriel H., and LeRoy H. Fischer. *Civil War Sites in Oklahoma.* Oklahoma City: Oklahoma Historical Society, 1967.

Articles/Papers

Alley, H.L. "Outlaw Treasure and Spanish Gold." *Treasure* 1, no. 6 (April 1971): 57.

Bahos, Charles. "On Opothleyahola's Trail: Locating the Battle of Round Mountains." *The Chronicles of Oklahoma* 63, no. 1 (Spring 1985): 58–89.

Boland, Judi. "Red River Shipwreck Reveals History." Oklahoman.com, October 12, 2003.

Burchart, Bill. "Lost Loot." *Oklahoma Today* 2, no. 12 (November 1977): 40–41.

Carter, Sharon. "Belle Starr's Iron Door." *Treasure Cache* (2003): 31–32.

Christopher, Gary W. "Has Part of the Reynolds Loot Been Found?" *Treasure World* 8, no. 11 (October–November 1974): 17–18.

Clark, Baxter Blue. "Opothleyahola and the Creeks During the Civil War." *Indian Leaders, Oklahoma's First Statesmen*, Oklahoma Historical Society (1979): 49–64.

Dearmore, B.F. "Spanish Fort Treasure." *Old West* 11, no. 5 (Fall 1976): 39.

Duffy, Howard M. "The Reynolds Gang's $100,000 Missing Outlaw Loot." *Treasure* 7, no. 12 (December 1976): 66–69.

Eckert, Jerry. "Behind the Iron Door: Lost Cache of the Wichita Mountains." *Treasure Cache* (1999): 50–54.

Emerson, Doyle. "Tales from Southeast Oklahoma." *Treasure* 23, no. 12 (December 1992): 62–63.

Ferrel, Bill. "Spanish Silver Found in Oklahoma." *Western Treasures* 6, no. 5 (December 1972): 34–36.

Foreman, Grant. "Reminiscences of Mr. R.P. Vann, East of Webbers Falls, Oklahoma." *The Chronicles of Oklahoma* 11, no. 2 (June 1933): 838–44.

Gaines, W. Craig. "Down the Drain." *Lost Treasure* 27, no. 3 (March 2002): 18–19.

———. "Dr. Hayes' Lost Gold." *Lost Treasure* 1, no. 9 (August 1976): 19.

———. "Farm Gold." *Lost Treasure* 26, no. 3 (March 2001): 19–20.

———. "Gold and Silver on the Arkansas River." *Lost Treasure* 41, no. 2 (February 2016): 9–10.

———. "Lost Ozark Mines." *Lost Treasure* 41, no. 4 (April 2016): 18–19.

———. "Oklahoma's Treasured Mountains." *Lost Treasure* 40, no. 9 (September 2015): 6–8.

———. "The Reynolds Gang Exposed." *Lost Treasure* 22, no. 8 (August 1997): 7–8.

———. "The Trader's Cache." *Lost Treasure* 40, no. 8 (August 2015): 18–19.

Getz, Donald E. "The Burro-Shoe Treasure of Jesse James." *Treasure World* 7, no. 5 (April–May 1973): 32–34, 39.

Grapes, W.W. "Treasure of Twin Mounds." *Lost Treasure* 2, no. 12 (November 1977): 40–41, 46–47.

Hardcastle, Stoney. "Mystery of Standing Rock—Buried Forever." *True West* 25, no. 3 (January–February 1978): 13, 53–54.

Henson, Michael Paul. "Lost Treasures in Oklahoma." *Lost Treasure* 5, no. 11 (October 1980): 40–43.

———. "Oklahoma—Gold! Gold! And Other Treasures." *Lost Treasure* 18, no. 6 (June 1993): 10, 12–13.
———. "Thousands of Years of Treasures Deposited in Oklahoma." *Lost Treasure* 9, no. 10 (October 1984): 47–50, 52–53.
Hilton, Tom. "Lost Civil War Gold." *True Treasure* 6, no. 6 (May–June 1972): 15–16.
———. "Treasure on Lee's Creek." *Treasure World* 4, no. 11 (October–November 1970): 30–31, 33–34, 36.
"The History and Legend of Devil's Canyon." *Treasure* 1, no. 2 (August 1970): 35–37, 46.
Holt, Benjamin. "Traders' Lost Mexican Silver." *True Treasure* 9, no. 4 (March–April 1975): 14–17.
Huddleston, B.A. "$80,000 Hoard in the Oklahoma Hills." *True Treasure* 3, no. 3 (May–June 1969): 27–29.
Jewell, Thomas B. "Mexican Gold in Oklahoma." *Lost Treasure* 2, no. 7 (June 1977): 56, 58.
Jones, Richard E. "Grandpa Clark's Gold." *Treasure Cache* (2004): 46–47.
Kelly, Bill. "Blood in the Red River Valley." *Lost Treasure* 21, no. 8 (August 1996): 8–11.
Lynn, Robert E. "Missing Gold in Oklahoma." *Treasure World* 8, no. 1 (December–January 1974): 35.
Mahan, Bill. "Buried Treasure Found." *Gold!* 3, no. 3 (Summer 1971): 7.
McKennon, C.H., and G.A.Y. "Chisholm Trail Treasure." *The Artifact* 1, no. 2 (March–April 1966): 10–11, 19.
Michael, Ralph. "A Record Breaking Day, Search for Murdering Martin's Buried Spoils Along Bird Creek." *Treasure Cache* (2001): 84–88.
Michaels, Jason (penname for W. Craig Gaines). "Cherokee Nation Treasures." *Lost Treasure* 27, no. 4 (April 2002): 36–38.
Nieberding, Velma. "Old Peoria: Mother of Mining Camps." *The Chronicles of Oklahoma* 50, no. 2 (Summer 1972): 142–55.
Oklahoma Parks & Resorts. "Robbers Cave State Park, Outlaw Hideout."
Packer, C.L. "Treasure Hunter with Know-How." *True West* 16, no. 2 (November–December 1968): 26–28, 60–63.
Padgett, Gary. "Lost Indian Territory Gold Cache." *Treasure World* 9, no. 5 (April–May 1975): 12–14.
Pallante, Anthony J. "Oklahoma: La Riviere La Mine." *Lost Treasure* 22, no. 6 (June 1997): 52–54.
Phipps, R.L. "Lost Gold Mines of Oklahoma." *The Chronicles of Oklahoma* 7 (September 1929): 341–43.

———. "A Pledge of Words Keeps in Secrecy Location of Lost Oklahoma Gold Mine." *The American Indian* 2, no. 2 (November 1927): 9.

Raymond, Ken. "Hunters Trail Jesse James' Gold Near Cement." Oklahoman.com, December 13, 2009.

Sasser, Charles W. "Jesse James' Missing Gold." *Lost Treasure* 42, no. 6 (June 2017): 24–26.

Smith, Buss. "Buried Loot at Red Rock." *True Treasure* 4, no. 8 (July–August 1973): 28–29, 32–33.

Smith, Walter R. "Some Legends of Oklahoma." *The Chronicles of Oklahoma* 4 (March 1926): 50–54.

Tisserand, Jacques. "Lost Choctaw Gold Mines." *True Treasure* 6, no. 10 (September–October 1972): 76–78.

———. "Missing Cache of Silver Dollars." *True Treasure* 4, no. 8 (July–August 1970): 39.

———. "Missing Half Bushel of Silver Coins." *True Treasure* 4, no. 8 (January–February 1972): 15–16, 18.

"Tom Hicks $600 Waits No More." *The Artifact* 2, no. 1 (February–March 1967): 26–27.

Townsend, Ben. "Bandit Loot in Northeast Oklahoma." *Gold!* (Spring 1976): 18–19.

———. "The Belle Star–Big Head Treasure." *True Treasure* 8, no. 10 (November–December 1973): 65–66.

———. "Caches of the Missouri Traders." *True Treasure* 8, no. 8 (July–August 1974): 12–13.

———. "Missing Loot of the Dalton Gang." *Lost Treasure* 1, no. 2 (January 1976): 11–14.

———. "Oklahoma's Camp Meeting Cache." *Treasure World* 8, no. 10 (October–November 1974): 41, 48.

Turpin, Robert F. "Belle Starr Hideout." *Treasure Hunt* 1, no. 2 (Summer 1974): 11.

———. "Bill Doolin's Kansas Loot." *Treasure Search/Found* 18, no. 10 (October 1990): 24–27, 49.

———. "Buffalo Head Williams Cache." *Treasure Hunt* 1, no. 2 (Summer 1974): 4.

———. "Eldorado's Spanish Gold." *Treasure Hunt* 1, no. 2 (Summer 1974): 5–7.

———. "Find Buried Treasure in Oklahoma." *Treasure* 8, no. 12 (December 1977): 52–55.

———. "German Shoemaker's Gold." *Treasure Hunt* 1, no. 2 (Summer 1974): 21.

———. "The Iron Door Treasure." *Treasure World* 6, no. 3 (February–March 1972): 28–31.
———. "Joe Payne's Silver Streak." *Treasure Hunt* 1, no. 2 (Summer 1974): 10.
———. "Lacy Mouse Gold Treasure." *Treasure Hunt* 1, no. 2 (Summer 1974): 8–9.
———. "Oklahoma Hot Spots." *Western Treasures* (August 1970): 34–36, 66.
———. "Robin Bobb's Treasure." *Treasure Hunt* 1, no. 2 (Summer 1974): 20.
———. "Spanish Gold in Oklahoma." *Treasure Hunt* 1, no. 2 (Summer 1974): 13.
———. "The Treasure of Locust Grove." *Treasure Hunt* 1, no. 2 (Summer 1974): 17.
Vance, Tom. "Outlaw Treasure in Lost City." *Lost Treasure* 31, no. 8 (August 2006): 48–49.
———. "The Real Treasure of Oklahoma's Wichita Mountains." *Lost Treasure* 5, no. 11 (October 1980): 54–58.
———. "Search for the $60,000 Indian Gold Cache." *Treasure* 9, no. 4 (April 1978): 42–44.
Villa, Benito. "Lost Gold of the Osage Hills." *Lost Treasure* 1, no. 12 (December 1975): 37–39.
Vincent, Melissa. "Robbers' Roost." The Encyclopedia of Oklahoma History and Culture, www.okhistory.org.
Wilson, Steve. "Cascorillo." *Treasure World* 3, no. 3 (August–September 1969): 27–29.
———. "Endless Quest for the Spider Rock Treasure." *Treasure World* 6, no. 9 (August–September 1972): 40–42, 47, 50–51.
———. "MISSING: 40 Jack Loads of Gold!" *Treasure World* 5, no. 3 (February–March 1971): 17.
———. "Missing Oklahoma Gold." *Treasure World* 5, no. 5 (April–May 1971): 39.
———. "Oklahoma's Missing Army Payroll." *True Treasure* 5, no. 4 (March–April 1971): 24–25.
———. "Oklahoma's Treasure Trails." *Saga's Treasure Special* 1, no. 1 (1970): 16–19, 54, 56–58.
———. "Outlaw's Lost Gold." *True Treasure* 5, no. 6 (May–June 1971): 36–38.
———. "Secrets of Devil's Canyon and Its Gold." *True Treasure* 3, no. 1 (January–February 1969): 54–65.
Wright, D. Buckley. "Buried Loot at Robber's Roost." *True Treasure* 7, no. 4 (March–April 1973): 22.

Zachary, Hugh. "Oklahoma's Cache of Southern Gold." *True Treasure* 2, no. 3 (March–April 1968): 32–35.

Websites

Lawmen.genealogyvillage.com
OKhistory.com.

Television Shows/Documentaries

America's Book of Secrets. Season 2, Episode 11, "Lost Treasures." 2013, The History Channel.

INDEX

D

E

F

G

H

I

J

K

L

M

N

O

P

Q

R

S

Y

ABOUT THE AUTHOR

The author as a five-year-old cowboy. *Author's photo.*

W. Craig Gaines is the author of *Great Lost Treasures Never Found*; *Hispanic Lost Treasure of the Eastern United States*; *Hispanic Treasures of the Western United States*; *The Confederate Cherokees: John Drew's Regiment of Mounted Rifles*; *Encyclopedia of Civil War Shipwrecks*; *Civil War Gold and Other Lost Treasures*; *Success in Life: 401 Encouraging Thoughts*; *Nostradamus' Curse*; and other books and articles. He has been interested in lost treasure since seeing the film *Treasure Island* when he was very young. He has written about one hundred published lost treasure stories for a variety of treasure hunting magazines over the years. Craig is an engineer, geologist and writer who has been in many of the areas mentioned in this work. He resides with his wife, Arla, in Tulsa, Oklahoma, and still searches for lost treasure.